GOOD NEWS STUDIES
Consulting Editor: Robert J. Karris, O.F.M.

Volume 12

Gospel Love

A Narrative Theology

by

John Navone, S.J.

 Michael Glazier, Inc.

Wilmington, Delaware

About the Author
John Navone, S.J., is Professor of Theology at the Gregorian University in Rome. He is internationally respected as an innovative theologian and author. Among his many publications are *Towards a Theology of Story; The Jesus Story: Our Life as Story in Christ;* and *Tellers of the Word: Nine Moments in the Theology of Story.*

First published in 1984 by Michael Glazier, Inc.
1723 Delaware Avenue, Wilmington, Delaware 19806

©1984 by Michael Glazier, Inc. All rights reserved.

Library of Congress Catalog Card Number: 84-81247
International Standard Book Number:
  Good News Studies: 0-89453-290-1
  GOSPEL LOVE: 0-89453-437-8

Typography by Richard Huber

Printed in the United States of America

For
James J. Hennesey, S.J.
David G. Schultenover, S.J.
Paul J. Shaughnessy, N.J.
Robert J. Spitzer, S.J.

Contents

Introduction 11

Chapter 1: Four Gospel Stories of God's Love 22
    I. Four Kerygmatic Stories 22
    II. Four Theological Stories 25
    III. Four Stories for Learning to "Know God" 27
    IV. Mark: Costly Commitment 30
    V. Matthew: Family Responsibilities 31
    VI. Luke: Outgoing Compassion 32
    VII. John: Mutual Indwelling 33
    VIII. Summary 35

Chapter 2: Jesus Living in God's Love 36
    I. The Synoptics 36
        1. The anger of Jesus 36
        2. The sadness of Jesus 38
        3. The compassion of Jesus 38
        4. The friendship of Jesus 40

    II. John's Gospel 41
        1. Jesus' love for a family 41
        2. Jesus' love for a disciple 42
        3. Jesus' love for all the disciples 42
        4. Jesus' love for all future believers 42
        5. God is Love 43

Chapter 3: Jesus Dying in God's Love 44
    Introduction 44

I. Mark ... 48
1. Two Points of View ... 48
2. Servant of God for All ... 49
3. The Eight Last Moments ... 50
4. The Blood of the Lamb ... 52
5. Three Hours of Darkness ... 53
6. Darkness Overcome ... 54
7. Passover Symbolism ... 54
8. Plague Symbolism ... 55
9. "Crying out with a loud voice" ... 56
10. Psalm of the Just One ... 57
11. The Torn Veil ... 58
12. The Temple Motif ... 59
13. A New Meaning for the Sacred ... 60
14. Breaking the Barriers ... 61
15. "I Am" ... 61
16. A House for All Nations ... 62
17. The Centurion: Voice of Faith ... 63
18. Mission Completed ... 64
19. The Cross Reveals ... 65

II. Matthew ... 66
1. "For the forgiveness of sins" ... 66
2. Eschatological Signs: Joel ... 66
3. Eschatological Signs: Ezechiel ... 67
4. The First to Benefit ... 68
5. Confession of Faith ... 70
6. Jesus: The Question ... 71
7. The Temptation and the Cross ... 73

III. Luke ... 75
1. An Exodus and an Ascension ... 76
2. The Innocent Martyr ... 78
3. The Torn Veil ... 80
4. Two Words of Mercy ... 81
5. The Final Word: Psalm 31 ... 83
6. The Temptation and the Cross ... 85

IV. John ... 86
1. Authority and Majesty ... 87

    2. Continuity and Climax 88
    3. Sending the Helper 91
    4. The New Community of Friends........... 92
    5. The Seamless Garment 94
    6. The Son's Love 95
    7. "I thirst" 96
    8. Trinitarian Love 99

Chapter 4: Reflections on Gospel Love 103

  I. Theological Reflection...................... 103
    1. The Hazard of Self-Deception 103
    2. The Authority of Love 104
    3. The Power of Love 106
    4. From Compassion to Passion 107
    5. The Quicksands of Self-Sufficiency 108
    6. "If you know these things"............... 108
    7. Freedom—Enabling Grace 109
    8. Struggle and Resistance 110
    9. Total Claims of the Kingdom 112
    10. "Happy to suffer for you" 113
    11. "That joy no one shall take from you" 114
    12. Befriending Love 115

  II. Principles and Practical Points of Reference... 117

Chapter 5: Why We Share the Good News:
     Lex Narrandi, Lex Credendi 122

Appendix 143

Indexes 154

INTRODUCTION

Gospel Love is a narrative theology; consequently, a word about my approach to narrative theology is in order.

There is more to story than just story; there is more to narrative theology than narratives. Narrative theology is not to be confused with the art of telling stories that one might acquire in a creative writing course for the preparation of homilies; rather, it is a Christian anthropology which is primarily concerned about our learning to know God, in the biblical sense of a covenant love relationship, through participation in the life of the crucified and risen Christ and his covenant community. If the Word of God incarnate is the life story of God, the narrative theologian will critically reflect on that story for learning to know God. The world of interiority, that realm of divine and human love at the integrating center of Jesus Christ's interpersonal life with all divine and human others, *his* knowing God, is expressed and communicated in the Gospel narratives, which are basically stories that we, too, might share that world and be fully transformed by it at the depths of our intra- and interpersonal and social lives. The narrative theologian critically reflects on the Gospel narratives with all the resources of his or her world of interiority, ever more fully to appropriate that of Jesus Christ for the achievement of human authenticity in the self-transcendence of Christian conversion both as event and life-long process. The Gospel narratives both express and address the world of conscious and intersubjective interiority for the radical transformation of human life at every level and in every dimension. This theologian employs the transcendental method and theory of Bernard Lonergan and Karl Rahner to mediate his understanding of the world of interiority expressed and communicated in the Gospel narratives. Even though there is no explicit reference made to them, their transcendental anthropology is operative throughout my narrative theology of the *lex narrandi, lex credendi* at the heart of our knowing the covenant-creating and covenant-sustaining God of the historical Judeo-Christian revelation by freely and responsibly choosing to live covenant-creating and covenant-sustaining lives of unrestricted and self-transcending covenant love for all (as opposed to covenant-destructive lives). Their transcendental anthropology is especially operative in my interpretation of the transformational character of the Gospel narratives as symbolizing four interrelated dimensions of human authenticity to be achieved in response to the grace and demand of God's unrestricted love and the realm of his transcendent love to which all humankind is constitutively oriented.

Some Lonerganian notions, which I shall not attempt here to explain, that are presuppositions for my narrative theology are the following. Human authenticity is achieved in self-transcendence; it is never a secure possession; it is ever a withdrawal from unauthenticity. The prior and immediate word that is God's gift of his love and the outer word of Scripture and our religious tradition which expresses it entails the religious effort towards authenticity in fidelity to God himself, drawing us to the realm of his transcendent love in and through his word. Lonergan's understanding of religious and Christian conversion, his intentionality analysis, his notion of faith as the knowledge born of religious love — all are central presuppositions of my approach to narrative theology.

Some Rahnerian notions that are presupposed in my narrative theology are the following. The categorical pertains to that dimension of human experience which is historically particular and concrete; the specific content of everyday knowledge and decision-making, as distinguished from its transcendental openness to the wholeness of being. Transcendence in human experience is the characteristic dynamism of the human spirit, whether in knowledge or in love or in freedom, to move beyond any particular or finite being toward a context or horizon (ultimately, God) which gives it final coherence and value. Our life stories and their narrative expressions reflect the transcendental-categorical structure of human consciousness. Our transcendental awareness, the world of our interiority, seeks objectification in external interaction with other persons and with our environment, with the tendency to manifest itself in all the dimensions of our life story. There is no purely spiritual, individual, unhistorical human life story; for we are bodily, social, and historical. Our various objectifications in concept, language, symbol, action, and such can never exhaust this transcendental dimension; they reflect it and can modify and intensify it. Even our most spiritual knowledge involves the work of imagination; there is no purely transcendental knowing for there is no thought without image. Our categorical experience is structured by these images and by their employment in our narratives. Our human development is facilitated by an improved imaginative formulation of who we are in the symbols and narratives which help to structure our experience because they represent true understandings of our historical experience. We are symbolizers. We not only employ symbols to express and structure our world in our narratives, but we are symbolic in our very constitution (life-story ground for our narrative interpretation). The human body is the symbol of the human spirit and its world of interiority. We possess an essential orientation to absolute mystery which is always present whether we explicitly recognize it or not and whether we accept it or reject it. Our genuine transcendental awareness will always and necessarily objectify itself in various degrees ranging from our feelings through narrative, and external action. The narrative quality of our complex experience of the Mystery that both pervades and transcends our lives, whether rightly or wrongly interpreted, inescapably contains a religious dimension that grounds narrative theology.

Knowing God (in the biblical sense), for Rahner, always rests upon the order of our love or disorder. It is not as if we first of all knew God in a *neutral* fashion, subsequently considering whether to adopt a loving or hating attitude towards Him. Such a neutral knowledge, such "objectivity," is an abstraction of the philosophers; for our concrete knowledge of God is always determined from the start by the way in which we love and treasure the things presented to us, including ourselves. On the basis of the Gospel truth Rahner affirms that accepting ourselves, we also accept Jesus, because in Jesus God has accepted us. Furthermore, in loving our neighbor we fulfill the law, because God Himself has become our neighbor, and so what is both nearest and transcendent at once is accepted and loved in every neighbor. Accepting responsibility for our neighbor and for ourselves before God evidences authentic covenant love and human maturity according to the spiritual pedagogy of the Judeo-Christian tradition. The stories of God of this tradition seek to inculcate and sustain such coresponsibility among the covenant people in order that they might truly learn to know God (in the biblical sense). "To be or not to be," in this tradition, is ultimately a question of knowing God in the community of his covenant-love. Telling the story of their lived experience of God's love is central to the liturgy of the covenant people, Jewish and Christian; they exist because God loves them; they have a life story whose origin, direction, and destiny is God Himself. Hearing God's word of love in one's own life story entails hearing that same word in the lives of one's covenant brothers and sisters of both past and present generations and of looking forward to the fulfillment of its promise. Revealed and communicated in Jesus Christ and the Gospel narratives is the God who is already and always, in the offer of his self-communication in the Holy Spirit of his love, in us as *the* question and *the* answer in one, even when they remain unspoken; therefore the proclamation of Jesus and the Gospel tells us only what we already *are* and what we are called to be under the sovereignty of God's unrestricted and universal love. As a narrative theologian, I am committed to a critical reflection on the interiority-objectivizing and interiority-communicating life story of Jesus Christ and his covenant brothers and sisters, expressed paradigmatically in the biblical narratives, with a view to knowing God (in the biblical sense) more deeply and having life most fully through the gift of his covenant-creating and covenant-sustaining love for all humankind.

The title of this book, *Gospel Love*, is inspired by a dictum of Wittgenstein, to the effect that if we claim to know something and cannot give a single example of it, perhaps we do not know what we are talking about. When the community of new covenant love claims to know God, it points to the Good News that is Jesus Christ, and affirms that "God is Love." This is what we mean by "love," human and divine; and we judge the authenticity of our lives in the light of that love; for there is nothing authentically human or divine apart from that.

Narrative theology is the sustained reflection of the theologian on the way we react to and appropriate the story of Jesus into our own stories. The life of Jesus and his community of faith is a story, the universal story of all human persons, whether they know it or not. Narrative theology is about human and divine subjects who relate to each other through telling and listening to the stories that make up the world in which we live. "Silence is golden" when it enables us to attend to Someone who speaks. If all telling of and listening to stories is a matter of relating, then the greatest story will be the greatest relating; the story that undergirds all other stories will be a story of universal and unrestricted love. Narrative theology attempts to underscore the self-investing love of God made manifest in Jesus, a love that creates, sustains, and brings to fulfillment all the partial, incomplete, and imperfect stories that we tell each other. When we withdraw completely from the world of loving relationships that make up a truly human life, we lapse into catatonia — a terrible, all-negating silence. In the Gospel stories Jesus makes the devils speak as a prelude to their being cast out. The image of a total silence, a total absence of storytelling and storylistening, is an image of absolute evil, the total negation of God, who, through Jesus and in the Spirit, is a Word spoken and a Love shared.

Narrative theology excludes any modernist or reductionist interpretation of theological anthropology, which seems to suggest that theological doctrines are to be viewed as statements about merely human realities. Rather, it is based on the position that humankind is for God, that religion is intrinsic to authentic humanism, and that in theology the theocentric and the anthropocentric coincide; so it is that all theological statements are to be matched by statements of their meaning in human terms. Narrative theology employs the category of story to bring to life theological truth through a contemporary apprehension of personal and social reality in all its concreteness. It aims to provide a wealth of new insights into what it means to be human.

I have chosen to write a narrative theology because I am convinced that all human stories are implicitly meant to communicate loving interpersonal and social relationships that ultimately are embraced by the value and mystery of a loving God. All human stories are meant to be "theological." We need theological stories because we are fundamentally interpersonal and because, if the Christian God's promise is true, we are fundamentally related to God as person. Since story is the only means by which our interpersonal and social reality can be expressed in its cognitive and affective fullness and since our relationship to God is fundamentally interpersonal and social, it follows that storytelling and storylistening provide the most appropriate means of enabling us to live this relationship. The Christian story celebrates life, living in, and being lived in by, the author of life. Being religious is living in the friendship of God, and sensing the fullness of life in His love. The heart of the Christian life is to dwell in the creative and sustaining love of God, and we express this indwelling in no other way than in loving God and our neighbor. Christian conversion, both as event and life-long process, is a story of learning how to dwell in a loving God who loves all. More precisely, it is a story of leaning how to let God be the loving God that He is by allowing Him to dwell within and among us, to enable us to give ourselves to each other in his love.

Three moments mark the journey that our readers will make through this book. The first moment is contained in the first two chapters. Our journey starts with the question, "What is love?" The Gospels are the Christian community's answer to that question. The answer is not an abstract definition, but the concrete story of Jesus' living and dying and rising in God's love. The Christian community proclaims the Good News that God is Love and loves everyone. It celebrates that community-creating love as the new life that God has poured out for all in the blood of the covenant (Mk 14:24; Mt 26:28; Lk 22:20). It experiences that love as the Spirit of God that is poured both into our hearts (Rm 5:5) and out upon all humankind (Acts 10:45). The Gospel writers want their readers to be transformed by the gift and demand of this love at every level of their being: intrapersonally, interpersonally, and socially. In the 17th century, Samuel Crossman wrote that Christ in his passion has

> "Love to the loveless shown
> That they might lovely be."

The story of God's unconditional love for us in Jesus Christ is the Christian community's norm for judging the authenticity of our own life and loves. It is the Good News of the Love that transcends every human love, given to us. It changes us from being unlovely to being lovely and loving by showing us what true loveliness could be. The four Gospels are four faces of God's love in Jesus Christ manifested as costly (Mark), fraternal (Matthew), universally compassionate (Luke), and inhabiting (John). God is where He acts. God's active presence in human hearts is manifested in deeds of compassionate, fraternal, and costly love for others. The Christian community employs its Gospels as a pedagogical resource for learning to "know God" by living and dying and rising in his love. They witness the community's conviction that our authenticity is a matter of ongoing growth in response to the gift of God's love. They imply our responsibility and possibility with respect to becoming what God in His love, as revealed in the crucified and risen Jesus, intends that we become: authentically loving persons, living under the sovereignty of God's love.

The story of the cross is the second moment of our journey. Whenever Jesus is asked what is the greatest commandment, or what is the way to eternal life, he sums up the whole of the law and the prophets in the two-fold commandment of love for God and one's neighbor. His own life of compassion reaches its end and climax in a death that is portrayed as an act of compassion, as a giving of his life for others. The events of the passion and death of Jesus bring to a climax a love that his disciples had known throughout his life. They express the meaning of his living and dying out of love for God and all others, as giving himself, as being broken and being poured out, as being servant.

I focus on the four accounts of the Passion as the key to understanding the meaning of that love and life which Jesus receives from his Father and communicates to us through their gift of the Spirit. The death of Jesus is the climax and culmination of his life: "Greater love than this no man has, than that a man lay down his life for his friends" (Jn 15:13). Jesus is most alive in the giving of his life. The cross is a symbol not of death, but of life even in death, of strength in weakness. Jesus gives his whole life. There is nothing more that he could give, no remainder left ungiven. This is the greatest act of giving, the greatest act of love of which one is capable, because it is final and definitive with no taking back.

To see Jesus is to see the Father. To see the meaning of Jesus' dying is to see the meaning of the Father's love going to the very limits of which love is capable within the particularities of a human life story. The death of Jesus was an act of living, not an act of dying. It is an affirmation of life even in the face of death. In this act of self-giving love, the community of Christian faith sees God and affirms that He is Love. It recognizes the gift and demand of God's love: "...that you love one another as I have loved you" (Jn 15:12).

The third moment of our journey turns from our contemplation of the Passion to the historical particularities of our intrapersonal, interpersonal, and social life stories, with the conviction that we are called to become actors — not mere onlookers — within Christ's story, sharing his life and his Spirit by dying and rising with him in the transforming power of the Father's love. When God begins his reign as Father in Jesus Christ, all things are made new in his love, all things are possible (Mk 10:27; 11:36; Mt 19:26; Lk 18:27). God's lordship in love is a creative goodness which makes others good. What does this mean for us today?

The fourth moment, or fifth chapter, is a theological reflection on that covenant love which is the basis for narrative theology. The authenticity of covenant love is manifested in both welcoming and telling the good news of God's love for us. The *lex narrandi* is the *lex credendi*.

Although the various gospels present different and complementary portraits of Jesus, I give more attention to Mark's passion narrative because it is foundational for the others; so much of what is predicated of his narrative holds for the others. Mark is the first to formulate Love's Good News in the form of a written gospel.

As an aid to grasping the cohesiveness of individual sections of the book, it may be useful to cross-reference particular pages. The material on the Son's love (pp. 95-96) is linked to Jesus' love for a family and a disciple (pp. 41-42). The discussion of "the many" (p. 106) should be joined to that of the "Servant of God for All" (pp. 49-50). The treatment of the relationship between compassion and passion (pp. 107-108) should look back to the compassion of Jesus (pp. 38-40). The study of knowledge in the fourth chapter (pp. 109-110) is related to the section on the gospels as stories for learning to know God (pp. 27-30). The presentation on befriending love (pp. 115-116) is related to the section on the friendship of Jesus (pp. 40-41).

A special bibliography invites the reader to go to the sources that inspired the writing of this book. Among these I am most indebted to Ernest Martinez, S.J. for the use of material from his unpublished doctoral dissertation on the gospel accounts of the death of Jesus, and to Albert Vanhoye, S.J. for his study of the passion accounts in the Synoptic Gospels.

The Revised Standard Version is the specific Bible translation used in the text.

Source Materials

B. Anderson, *Out of the Depths*, Philadelphia: Westminster Press, 1974.

P. F. Bradshaw, *Daily Prayer in the Early Church*, London: SPCK, 1981.

T. H. Groome, *Christian Religious Education*, San Francisco: Harper & Row, 1980.

J. D. Kingsbury, *Matthew*, Philadelphia: Fortress Press, 1977.

W. H. Kelber, Ed., *The Passion of Mark: Studies on Mark 14-16*, Philadelphia: Fortress Press, 1976.

_____, *Jesus Christ in Matthew, Mark, and Luke*, Philadelphia: Fortress Press, 1981.

X. Léon-Dufour, "Recits de la Passion," *Dictionnaire de la Bible* 35 (1960) cols. 1410-92.

E. Martinez, *The Gospel Accounts of the Death of Jesus*, Rome: unpublished dissertation for the Theology Faculty of the Gregorian University, 1969.

J. Navone, *Themes of St. Luke*, Rome: Gregorian University Press, 1970.

J. Navone and Thomas Cooper, *Tellers of the Word*, New York: Le Jacq, 1981.

J. B. Segal, *The Hebrew Passover: From the Earliest Times to A.D. 70*, London: Oxford University Press, 1963.

D. J. Selby, *Introduction to the New Testament*, New York: Macmillan, 1971.

E. Trocmé, *The Passion as Liturgy: A Study in the Origin of the Passion Narratives in the Four Gospels*, London: SCM Press, 1983.

A. Vanhoye, *Structure and Theology of the Accounts of the Passion in the Synoptic Gospels*, trs. by C.H. Giblin, Collegeville, MN: Liturgical Press, 1967.

A. Vanhoye, I. de la Potterie, C. Duquoc, E. Charpentier, *La Passione secondo i quattro Vangeli*, Brescia: Editrice Queriniana, 1983.

S. Zedda, *L'amore di Cristo nel nuovo testamento*, Rome: Apostolato della Preghiera, 1981.

Jerome Biblical Commentary, R. E. Brown, J. A. Fitzmyer, R. E. Murphy, Eds., Englewood Cliffs, NJ: Prentice-Hall, 1968.

1. FOUR GOSPEL STORIES OF GOD'S LOVE

I. Four Kerygmatic Stories

The four Gospels are four versions of the Jesus story. Each is a "story" in the sense that each presents a narrative account of the earthly ministry of Jesus of Nazareth. The narrative mode constitutes the founding medium of Christian religious perception, first in the narratives of Jesus himself (parables), then in the *kerygma* (proclamation, announcement, preaching) of the early Church and later in the Gospels. The significance of narrative (story) in the Judeo-Christian perception is suggested by Amos Wilder: "God is an active and purposeful God and his action with and for man has a beginning, middle and an end like any good story."[1]

The Gospel writers tell a kergymatic story that is of the nature of "good news" or "proclamation"; for Jesus is unlike other persons who have died and are gone. By virtue of his resurrection, Jesus is not dead but lives. The earthly Jesus of the Gospel story is one with the risen Jesus whom his

---

[1] Amos Wilder, *The Language of the Gospel* (New York: Harper and Row, 1964), p. 64. Narrative is the relating of an event in which there is a buildup (desis) and a release (lysis) of tension, or, to define it in an equally broad sense, a plot with a beginning, a middle, and an end. Narrative is an account of events, whether actual or fanciful, reported in any way for any reason.

community encounters in its prayer and preaching and teaching. The story proclaims a saving event: "It pleased God by the foolishness of *the preaching* to save them that believe" (1 Cor 1:21). The story is punctuated with references to Old Testament prophecy concerning the fulfillment of the age with Christ as its Lord, the fact of Jesus' powers and preaching, his crucifixion, resurrection, and exaltation, the promise of his coming, the call to repentance and the offer of forgiveness. The Gospel of Mark is the *kerygma* briefly elaborated, beginning with prophecy and ending with the promise of a Christophany; it is the saving message of the saving event.[2] Each Gospel writer tells the story of the promise and claims of that event.

The interest of the early Christian witness to Jesus lay in religious conversion. Early Christian preaching aimed to communicate the "good news" of the Jesus story, the acceptance of which entailed a personal transformation (*metanoia* or conversion) on the part of the hearers. Christian preaching proclaimed religious conversion, thematized under the rubric of becoming a disciple of Jesus, as the authentic fulfillment of our humanity. Under the concrete conditions of human existence this fulfillment was also presented as redemptive, that is, as the solution to the problem of evil.

The kerygma, both as the content of what is preached and the act of preaching, provides the basic framework for the Gospel story. The witness to Jesus is good news for all; the call to follow Jesus promises authentic fulfillment and redemption. The evangelists recount the words and deeds of Jesus to prompt, foster, and nourish faith in their hearers. From the many accounts of Jesus' words and deeds, which the apostles have used in their preaching, the evangelists select those which they need and arrange them in such a way that they will achieve their goal of preaching to the Christian

---

[2]In the New Testament kergyma can refer to the content, event and office of proclamation. In contrast to teaching (*didache*) which expresses the revelation of Christ conceptually and logically in doctrines, the emphasis of the kerygma falls on public proclamation and the promise and claims of the saving event.

community. The witness to Jesus formed the content of the preaching, and its intent was directed to religious conversion. The preaching announced Jesus' destiny, that he died and was raised, and it affirmed the importance of Jesus for others. The preaching continues Jesus' call to conversion, to unconditional trust in the Father. Whatever their differences in outlook, emphasis or depiction of Jesus, the evangelists share the same kerygmatic motive. Mark's graphic portrayal of Jesus as the suffering Messiah, for example, differs from Matthew's image of Jesus as the fulfillment of Israel's hopes. Luke's picture of Jesus as the champion of the poor, outcasts and sinners varies slightly from the first two. If John knew the Gospel of Mark, as seems quite likely, then he used its content with a freshness of outlook and a breadth of vision unmatched by either Matthew or Luke; he has given us the Gospel of Love, in which Jesus is the Word of the Father's love for humankind. In substance, however, the four are kerygmatically the same: Jesus' life and death and destiny fulfill God's plan for all humankind.

The kerygmatic aim underlying the New Testament writings generated a massive effort to convince people of the meaning Christian faith found incarnate in Jesus and to persuade them to accept and to live out the values inherent in that meaning. This effort implied the task of the Christian imagination of bringing to full expression and linguistically articulating the meaning incarnate in Jesus. To express and communicate Jesus' identity forcefully, those who contributed to the formative tradition of the New Testament constructed dramatic narratives. Motivated by their kerygmatic interest in conversion and redemption, they enriched and reshaped their memories of Jesus' words and deeds with appropriate images drawn from the Hellenistic world and above all from the Old Testament. The crucified and risen Jesus became the Messiah, the Suffering Servant, the Lord, the Son of Man. Each image placed at the service of Christian faith a wealth of symbolic power evoking the meaning incarnate in Jesus.

The New Testament witness to Jesus symbolizes the realm of the transcendent to which we are constitutively oriented. When converted subjects hear the New Testament read in liturgical celebration or when they devote themselves to private meditation on it, they accept its proclamation as God's Word. This word thematizes their religious conversion, the unrestricted love which they have received and accepted as the integrating center of their lives. Through the dramatic narratives and images of the New Testament, they learn to identify the ultimate source and term of that love as the Father of Jesus Christ, the God of Israel who has sent his Son among us. Jesus, the revelation of the Father, completes his mission by sending the Spirit. Thus the New Testament symbolizes the realm of the transcendent in Trinitarian imagery which interprets that realm in interpersonal terms.

II. Four Theological Stories

The New Testament witness thematizes the significance of its central and controlling image — the crucified and risen Jesus — by placing it in a dramatic narrative. Jesus' death and destiny fulfill God's plan for creation. The opposition to Jesus manifested by his enemies casts his death as the fate of the innocent one. Jesus persists in challenging his opponents with an unconditional affirmation of the truth and answers evil with a love rooted in that of God. Although this leads to the cross, the New Testament affirmation of the resurrection implies that such a life was not futile. God vindicates it. The New Testament proclaims that by accepting death out of love, Jesus went on to further life. By accepting death as the culminating of the resistance of evil to his words and deeds of love, Jesus became a source of life to those who would accept his words and perform similar deeds. The New Testament invites its hearers to follow Jesus through death to resurrection with the firm conviction that such self-sacrificing love will not prove futile. Such love, rooted in that of God, is invincible. Its transforming power enables the process of self-transcendence in a new life that is the fullness of human living flowing from fidelity to the demands of Christian conversion.

The New Testament writers are men of the Church who recount what the Church experienced in faith about the meaning of Jesus' life, death, and resurrection. They are men of faith writing to persons of faith, trying to build up the faith of the Christian community. By conveying symbolically the meaning incarnate in Jesus, the New Testament writers supply a basis of meaning upon which religiously converted persons may and in fact do make common judgments and decisions about what Christians are to believe, what they are to become, and what they are to do. They recount the Church's preaching and teaching about Jesus, its worship of and faith in Jesus, making an appeal for conversion on a level prior to that on which doctrinal systems and organized institutions arise. They seek to transform human subjectivity and interiority by communicating Jesus' message and meaning.

Everything that the Evangelists write about the story of God in Jesus Christ and his community of faith has an historical, theological, and hortatory aim. We must not assume a plain historical, or doctrinal, or moral meaning in any passage of the Gospel story. If the interpreter plunges in one direction, he or she has a two-thirds chance of being wrong! The Good News that is Jesus Christ embodies the true meaning and value of what we are called to become through the grace and demand of God. The true goodness of the Gospel story has a double reference: to the world *behind* the text (the events in the life, preaching, and paschal mystery of Jesus' dying and rising), and to the world *in front of* the text (the real possibilities for self-understanding and transformation that, when realized, constitute Christian discipleship and the coming of the Kingdom).

The proclamation and the promise and claims of the saving event that is Jesus Christ (kerygma) are related to the strongly exhortatory content of the Gospel story "to go and to do likewise," which is termed paraenetic. Paraenesis refers to all exhortations and encouragement of an ethical and practical nature; it ranges over various topics (e.g. love,

Gal 5:13-14; marriage, fidelity, and celibacy, 1 Cor 7; interpersonal relationships, Rom 12:19-21; 14:1—15:7, and so on). Kerygma and paraenesis are related to each other as gift and task, indicative and imperative, grace and demand, and in the realm of theological reflection as dogmatics and ethics. The promise and claim of God in Jesus Christ and the gift of his Holy Spirit are the foundation for the paraenetic intention of the four kerygmatic and theological stories. The Good News that is Jesus Christ both reveals and demands what we are called to become under the sovereignty of God's love.

III. Four Stories for Learning to "Know God"

Evangelization, catechetics, and prayer are three dimensions of Christian conversion and life in the church that condition the formation of the Gospel tradition. They are three dimensions of life in the community that results from the outer communication of Christ's message and from the inner gift of God's love. Evangelization is an apostolic mission in which the church reaches out to those who have not heard the Gospel of God concerning his Son; catechesis is a pastoral mission in which the church enlightens those who have been evangelized in order that they might live as responsible adult Christians; prayer is a function of the church in which Christians individually and communally turn to God the Father, who grants them new life in Jesus Christ their Lord and in the gift of the Holy Spirit. The Gospel writers' concerns are both informational and transformational. The message tells what is to be believed; it crystallizes the inner gift of love into overt Christian fellowship; it directs Christian service to human society to bring about the kingdom of God.

New Testament passages with a strong exhortatory content (paraenesis) express the transformational intention of Christ's message. The kerygma and paraenesis, the informational and transformational, are related to each other as gift and task, indicative and imperative, and in the realm of theological reflection as dogmatics and ethics. The promise of the Gospel truth is the foundation and presupposition of the claims of paraenesis (exhortation, advice, counsel). Paul, for example, admonishes the believers to become what the faith declares them to be already in Christ (cf. Rom 6:1-14; 8:12-13; 1 Cor 5:7-8; 6:9-12, 15-20, etc.) Concrete pastoral advice for specific situations is given in 1 and 2 Cor. and Phil. Didactic materials in the Gospels can be traced to the situation of baptismal instruction, which included both the formal contents of faith and the ethical rules derived therefrom: "if you know these things, blessed are you if you do them" (Jn 13:17).

The New Testament writers want their hearers to know God with the knowledge that is grounded in love and right action (cf. Phil 1:9ff.). To "grow in the knowledge of God," one must "lead a life worthy of the Lord and pleasing to him in every way..." (Col 1:10). For the New Testament writers "knowing God" is grounded in a loving relationship and leads to loving service for others. God is known by those who acknowledge his sovereignty in mind and heart, by those who do his will. To "know God" is to love, to obey, to believe, and to hope. John affirms that "the man without love has known nothing of God" (1 Jn 4:8). Knowledge and love of God and of Christ grow together and do not exist apart. This knowing and loving includes one's neighbor: "Whoever loves God must also love his brother" (1 Jn 4:21). Self-sacrificing and self-investing love for others arises from and expresses our acceptance of the love that God has given us in his Son and Spirit: "Beloved, if God has loved us so, we must have the same love for one another" (1 Jn 4:11; also Jn 13:34; 15:12). There is no "knowing God" apart from loving God and neighbor. Furthermore, such knowing and loving are not passive. "Knowing God" does not mean the knowledge of investigation, observation or speculation, nor of mystical vision remote from historical commitments or action; rather, it is measured in the deeds by which we follow Jesus in self-sacrificing love for our neighbor in response to his injunction to love God above all: "The way we can be sure of our knowledge of him is to keep his commandments"

(1 Jn 2:3). The disobedient person does not know God: "The man who sins has not seen him or known him" (1 Jn 3:6; also 1 Jn 2:3-5). "Knowing God" means the activity of believing and trusting, of being actively committed in loving obedience to doing his will for oneself and others. "Do you know God?" is the Gospel question for everyone.

Not to "know God," in the biblical tradition, is to be less than human. The person without faith and hope and trust and love does not know God; such a person is in a dreadful state of brutishness, emptiness, and folly. The biblical authors find that there is something radically wrong with the person who does not adore, reverence, thank, and praise God. The prophets warned that the worshiper is assimilated to the object of his or her worship: "Emptiness they worshiped, emptiness they became" (Jer 2:5). Punishment is meted out for the person "who knows not God" (Job 18:21). The failure to "know God" connotes a loss of humanity on the individual and social levels, a radical infidelity to the exigences of self-transcendence in religious conversion (which has an intrinsic and organic connection with the rest of human self-transcendence in moral and intellectual conversion). The failure to "know God" results in an undeveloped, biased, and distorted self and society.

The way we treat others is an index for our "knowledge" of God: "He did what was right and just, and it went well with him. Because he dispensed justice to the weak and the poor, it went well with him. Is this not true knowledge of me? says the Lord" (Jer 22:15-16). "Knowing" God involves doing God's will for oneself and others; it benefits others, no less than ourselves. How seriously we take others reflects how seriously we take God.

Even where there is the religious belief and commitment of "knowing" God, we may be hindered in various ways from attaining the complete surrender that is the fulness of religious conversion. The response to the grace and demand of God's transforming and fulfilling will involves tension between the self as transcending and the self as transcended, between authenticity and unauthenticity, between "knowledge" and "ignorance" of God, within the human reality of individuals and groups. The Gospel writers implicitly recognize this tension in conversion as lived; consequently, the Gospels are rich in pedagogical resources for encouraging their readers to deepen their "knowledge" of God and to overcome their ignorance of Him by following Jesus Christ in receiving and accepting the grace and demand of the Father's love as the integrating center of their lives. The Gospel writers tell the story of Jesus that we might "know God" by seeking and doing His will for ourselves and others within the historical particularities of our lives.

The way each Gospel writer tells the story of Jesus calls our attention to particular aspects of "knowing God" in following Jesus Christ within his community of faith. The Gospel writers complement one another in their summons to follow Jesus Christ for the attainment of human fulfillment under the sovereignty of God's loving will for all in the kingdom.

IV. MARK: Costly Commitment

The Gospel of Mark summons us to a life of following in the way of a crucified Lord: "If any man would come after me, let him deny himself and take up his cross and follow me. For whoever would save his life will lose it, and whoever loses his life for my sake and the gospel's will save it" (8:34-35). Commitment to the Father's will for ourselves and others entails the suffering of overcoming self-will. "Not my will, but thine," (14:37), Jesus prayed in perfect self-surrender. The Son of God experiences the suffering of utter self-abandonment to his Father's will for himself and all others: "My God, my God, why have you forsaken me?" (15:34). If the disciple is to enter into the fulness of life that belongs to his risen Lord, he must also, like his Lord, experience the suffering of self-denial that is entailed in perfect fidelity to seeking and fulfilling the Father's will for ourselves and others. The sacrifice is worthwhile because we shall never know what God's love is like without it. This is the truly "Good News" that God's way of living and loving can be ours, if only we accept the invitation of Jesus: "Repent and believe the Good News" (1:15). Inasmuch as the Father's will is for the supreme good of all (the fullness of life and love in his kingdom), following the suffering Son of Man in his total commitment to that will is for the service of all: "Whoever would be great among you must be your servant, and whoever would be first among you must be slave of all. For the Son of Man came not to be served but to serve, and to give his life as a ransom for many" (10:43-45).

Jesus Christ is the agent of God's will for the coming of his rule in love for all in the kingdom (1:15). Because God's will for him is his will for all, Jesus' total commitment to God is for the good (service or ransom) of all (10:43-45 and 14:24). All are called to be with him under the sovereignty of God's love in the kingdom. God creates and sustains and destines a universe to become his kingdom through the agency of Jesus Christ; therefore, God's will for the good of the individual is for the good of all. God alone knows and loves all from the beginning to the end of time; therefore, the fulfillment of life in the kingdom of his love for all is totally and exclusively his doing.

V. *MATTHEW: Family Responsibilities*

The Gospel of Matthew summons us to life in the family of Jesus, the risen and exalted Son of God who presides over and resides in his church (28:19-20; also 1:23; 18:20). Jesus designates his disciples as "sons of God" (5:9), "sons of your heavenly Father" (5:45), and "sons of the kingdom" (13:38). Jesus declares that his disciples are his true relatives (12:49) and his "brothers" (28:10), and tells the disciples that they, too, are all "brothers" (23:8; also 18:21, 35). Matthew has Jesus stress at once his uniqueness in comparison with his disciples and his "relatedness" to them: "For whoever does the will of *my Father* in heaven is *my brother, and sister, and mother*" (12:50).

Matthew portrays Jesus' unique relationship with God (cf. 11:25-27). God is the Father of Jesus in a way not predicated of other human beings (1:22-23; 2:15; 3:17; 11:27; 17:5). Conversely, Jesus is the Son of God in a manner that is true of no one else (3:16-17; 11:27; 14:33; 16:16; 26:63-64; 27:54; 28:19). Nevertheless, when Jesus calls persons to follow him, Matthew shows that through him, the Messiah Son of God, they enter into a relationship of sonship with God. The Christians of Matthew's community know themselves to be "sons of God" and "brothers" of Jesus and of one another. As sons of God, they are also the "little ones," for they recognize that they are totally dependent upon their heavenly Father (18:3, 6, 10). As brothers of Jesus and of one another, they are at the same time the "servants" and "slaves" of one another (20:25-28). And as the followers of Jesus, they are likewise "disciples" (e.g. 8:23), for they have taken upon themselves his yoke and they "learn" from him (11:29; also, 10:24-25). It is Jesus who summons, dispatches, commands, and teaches, and it is they who follow, go, obey, and heed. The Matthaean community is a brotherhood of the sons of God and the disciples of Jesus. Through his presence Jesus, the earthly and exalted Son of God, mediates to his disciples or church the gracious, saving presence of God and his rule (1:23; 18:20; 28:20).

VI. LUKE: *Outgoing Compassion*

The Gospel of Luke summons us to follow Jesus in showing compassion for others and so become with him "children of the Most High" (6:35), manifesting the life of God among humankind. Compassionate love for others is, for Luke, the perfection of divine and human life. Where Matthew has Jesus demand, "You must be perfect just as your heavenly Father is perfect" (5:48), Luke has Jesus specify the meaning of perfection: "Be compassionate as your Father is compassionate" (6:36). Such compassion is more than an emotion of sympathy or benevolence; it encompasses the concrete doing of good for others out of a love that is rooted in God. Compassionate love is devoid of self-interest and considers only the need of its recipients, not their attitude to the giver, nor their deserts, because it derives from God, who is kind even to the ungrateful and the wicked (6:35). Jesus demands that love must be given where none is given in return, benefits conferred where none are deserved (6:32-34). Jesus' words and deeds, his life and death, of compassionate love for all without limits or conditions, express the universal scope of God's saving will. The universal scope of God's compassion is implied in the context of Jesus' journey to Jerusalem, when the question is asked about those who will be saved (13:23). Jesus answers that the first (Jews) shall be last and that the last (Gentiles) shall be first (13:30). All peoples, Jews and Gentiles, are invited to form the messianic kingdom (13:29). Jesus expresses the community-creating character of God's compassionate love for all in his deep concern for outcasts, sinners, and Samaritans (See 5:1-11; 7:36-38; 9:51-55; 10:29-37; 17:11-19; 18:9-14; 19:1-10; 23:39-43). Jesus announces that his meals with sinners are an anticipatory token of what God intends to do, that is, to receive sinners at his heavenly table (5:29-32; 15:1-2; 19:5-7).

To inherit the eternal life of the kingdom (10:25), Jesus demands the compassionate love that helps others (10:30-37). Fidelity to Jesus' demand is self-surrender to God's compassionate love in Jesus. Eternal life is even now leading us to be compassionate and do good for others.

VII. JOHN: *Mutual Indwelling*

The Gospel of John summons us to eternal life and friendship in Christ: "These (signs) are written that you may believe that Jesus is the Christ, the Son of God, and that believing you may have life in his name" (20:31). In Jesus Christ we have been given the gift of eternal life: "And this is eternal life, that they may know thee the only true God, and Jesus Christ whom thou hast sent" (17:3). This "knowledge" is not just an abstract intellectual exercise, but an intimate personal relationship that is described as mutual indwelling: "Do you not believe that I am in the Father and the Father in me?" (14:10). Jesus extends his mystical communion with his Father to his friends. Just as he dwells in the Father, so his friends dwell in him: "As the Father has loved me, so have I loved you; abide in my love" (15:9). Eternal life is mystical union joined to the highest personalism. We dwell in Jesus; Jesus dwells in the Father; we all dwell in one another. We are completely one with God and others and the universe; and yet we become our truest selves, reaching the apex of human personalism and authenticity.

The life which that knowledge of "the only true God, and Jesus Christ whom thou hast sent" begets is a life of love that has its imperative: "if you love me, you will keep my commandments" (14:15). The "commandments" are reducible to one: "This is my commandment that you love one another as I have loved you" (15:12). The Passion defines the meaning of love, of how Jesus loved us: "Greater love has no man than this, that a man lay down his life for his friends" (15:13). The mystical indwelling of Jesus and his Father is the eternal life that reaches out to embrace all others through the gift of the Holy Spirit: "I will pray the Father and he will give you another Counsellor to be with you forever, that Spirit of Truth..."(14:15-16). Eternal life is the interpersonal life of reciprocal love between the Father and the Son that is even now manifested in the fraternal love of Christians who dwell in one another (17:21, 26; also 13:35).

As Jesus is Son by nature, we are sons or daughters by adoption. As he dwells in the Father, we dwell in the Father; as he dwells in us, we dwell in one another. This love of mystical indwelling is not sterile but creative. Jesus affirms that his words and deeds are those of his Father who dwells in him (14:10). Similarly, the mutual indwelling of Jesus and his disciples is creative: "He who abides in me, and I in him, he it is that bears much fruit..." (15:5). God's eternal life of interpersonal love is the community-creating reality that is given to us in Jesus Christ and his community of faith: "No longer do I call you servants...But I have called you friends, because all things I have heard from my Father I have made known to you" (15:15). Eternal life is eternal friendship, made available to all through Jesus' laying down his life for his friends (15:13). The Gospel of John is a summons to the Eternal Friendship which Jesus Christ reveals to be the origin and ground and destiny of every human life. It proclaims that God's indwelling love is the source and motive and momentum for our free and costly commitment to others.

VIII. SUMMARY

The Gospels summon us to authentic human development under the sovereignty of God's love of outgoing compassion and friendship for all that is revealed and communicated in the crucified and risen Jesus Christ and his community of faith. They serve the purpose of grace and the demand of God's transcendent love for human fulfillment. They articulate and objectify in narrative form the meaning and value and demands of this love for us, both as individuals and as a community, that we may become what God intends us to be within his universal story of unfolding love. The Father's love for us is the source of our responsibility with regard both to the absolutely Other (God) and to all others. What we have to give is God's love. Our receptivity is the ground of our productivity in sharing Christ's life of service, his shaping of the future into the form of the kingdom. The greatest in the kingdom, therefore, is the one most dependent upon and most responsive to the Father's love (cf. Mt. 18:1-7, 10): Jesus Christ, the Son of God, whose receptivity and responsibility make the fellowship-creating mystery of the Father's love available to all humankind.

The self-transcending love of the Father and Son is eternal life and friendship in the kingdom of God. It is manifest in Jesus Christ's suffering out of love in commitment to his Father's will for himself and the ransom of all others. It is manifest when the fellowship-creating reality of the messianic community brings forth the fruits of the kingdom (Mt 21:43) that glorify the Father (Mt 5:16), both in the compassionate service of one another and of all humankind.

2. JESUS LIVING IN GOD'S LOVE

Jesus Christ reveals that God is Love. We shall consider some of the forms that God's love for us takes in Jesus Christ as presented in the four Gospels. Such a consideration can help to free us from a univocal understanding of Christian love, inasmuch as God's love takes many forms in the life and death of his beloved Son. The Synoptic writers' portrait of Jesus enables us to grasp at least four of the distinctive forms: anger, sadness, compassion, and friendship.

I. The Synoptics

1. *The anger of Jesus.* Jesus shows anger at the heartlessness of the Pharisees (Mk 3:5), whose legalistic interpretation of the sabbath day would prevent both good deeds and the saving of life. Reproving them, Jesus cures the man with a withered hand in a synagogue on the sabbath: "Then, grieved to find them so obstinate, he looked angrily round at them, and said to the man, 'Stretch out your hand.'" Jesus angrily addresses the Pharisees as "brood of vipers" in Matthew's Gospel (12:34; 23:33). Their words and deeds manifest their evil hearts.

Jesus puts angry words in his own mouth when he represents himself as judge (Mt 7:23; 24:51; Lk 12:46; 13:27). He is angry when his disciples turn away the little children that people were bringing to him:"... when Jesus saw this he was indignant" (Mk 10:14). He manifests his wrath in the cleansing of the Temple (Mk 11:15-17; Mt 21:12-13; Lk 19:45-46; Jn 2:13-17). Jesus "sternly warned" the two men whose blindness he cured to say nothing about it to anyone (Mt 9:30). He "sternly ordered" the leper whom he had cured to do the same (Mk 1:43). He rebukes his disciples for their lack of faith: "Have you no faith?" (Mk 4:40); "Do you not yet perceive or understand? Are your hearts hardened? Having eyes do you not see, and having ears do you not hear? And do you not remember?" (Mk 8:18). He sharply rebukes Peter for failing to understand why he must suffer and die as Messiah: "Get behind me, Satan! For you are not on the side of God, but of men" (Mk 8:33). Luke's account of the disciples on the road to Emmaus portrays a similar reproof: "You foolish men! So slow to believe the full message of the prophets! Was it not ordained that the Christ should suffer and so enter into his glory?" (24:25-26). The kingdom comes in God's grace *and* its costly demand.

Jesus condemns the unrepentant towns (Mt 11:20-21), and curses the barren fig tree (Mk 11:21). His anger and indignation are the sign and incarnation of God's redemptive activity (Mt 12:34; 15:7; 23:13-36; Mk 3:5; 9:42; 10:14; Lk: 10:13,15; 9:41). His anger, like that of the God of Israel, expresses the demands of the covenant for fidelity and righteousness. The God of Israel is a jealous God whose love excludes all other gods, or idols. What Israel predicated of God's wrath is incarnated in Jesus (see Rom 1:18) and his ministry for the salvation of all human persons. The anger of Jesus expresses the liberating and all-encompassing Love that he reveals as God. He is angry with the disciples, who wished to keep the children away from him, because he loved the children: "He put his arms around them, laid his hands on them and gave them his blessing" (Mk 10:16). His anger, because it proceeds from the God who is Love, never harms or destroys human persons; rather, it frees and blesses them.

2. *The sadness of Jesus.* As the "man of sorrows" (cf. Mt. 26:37; Mk 14:34; Lk 19:41; 22:44; John 11:35), Jesus recalls the Suffering Servant of the Lord of Isaiah 52:13 - 53:12 (cf. Mt 8:17; Lk 22:37). Jesus experiences profound inner anguish: "In his anguish he prayed even more earnestly, and his sweat fell to the ground like great drops of blood" (Lk 22:44). He was distressed by the hard-hearted Pharisees (Mk 3:5). He lamented Jerusalem's unawareness of the hour of its visitation (Lk 19:41); for he profoundly loved his Jewish people. He was "sad to the point of dying" (Mt 26:37-38); yet, he uses the confident psalm of the persecuted just one when he feels the pain of abandonment in dying on the cross (Mt 27:46). His trust in God pervades a sorrow that never overcomes it. He hands himself over to the one who seems to forsake him (Lk 23:46). Matthew underscores the sorrow of Jesus in his passion narrative, where Mark and Luke emphasize his agony (Mk 14:33; Lk 22:44). Jesus' filial love of his Father, the source of his fraternal love for all others, enabled him to accept the depths of sadness, sorrow, and anguish willingly for the salvation of all (cf. Mk 10:45; Mt 20:28). Because he loved his Father and all others, he was liable to suffering the utmost sadness in witnessing others betray their true selves in rejecting his Father's love for them and others. He wept over Jerusalem with the love that grieves over the self-destruction of the beloved. The fulness of the Father's love did not make him immune to sorrow over the self-destruction of others; rather, it made him profoundly liable to the very depths of sadness.

3. *The compassion of Jesus.* Jesus' weeping over Jerusalem (Lk 19:41) expresses both sadness and compassion. The Greek verb for compassion-mercy-love (*splanchnizomai*) appears only in the Synoptic Gospels, where it refers directly to Jesus nine times and indirectly three times, when it refers to parables that speak of the mercy of God and of Jesus.

Jesus is moved to compassion at the sight of a leper, whom he cures (Mk 1:41). Matthew and Luke recount the same event without noting the feeling of Jesus for the afflicted leper. Mark uses the same word for compassion (*splanchnistheis*) when he has the father of the epileptic son ask Jesus to have compassion and to help (Mk 9:23).

Jesus feels compassion for the crowds because they were harassed and dejected, like sheep without a shepherd (Mt 9:36). Just before his first miracles of the loaves, he sees a large crowd; he has compassion for them and heals their sick (Mt 14:14; Mk. 6:34). At his second multiplication of the loaves, both Matthew and Mark have Jesus express his compassion for the crowd (Mt 15:32; Mk 8:2). Although Luke omits any mention of compassion in his single account of the event (Lk 9:10-17), he employs the word with reference to the widow of Nain: "When the Lord saw her he felt compassion for her" (7:13).

Luke employs the word for compassion (*splanchnizomai*) in two parables which reflect the spirit of Jesus. The Good Samaritan is moved to compassion at the sight of the man left to die (Lk 10:33). Jesus concludes the parable with the injunction: "Go and do likewise" (10:37). In the parable of the Lost Son ("Prodigal Son"), the father is moved to compassion at the sight of him, while he is still a long way off (Lk 15:20). The introduction to this parable, one of three on mercy, indicates that Jesus identifies his own compassion for sinners with that of his Father (Lk 15:1-2). In the parable of the unforgiving debtor, Matthew describes the master as moved to compassion by his servant's misery (Mt 18:27,33).

Luke's canticle of Zechariah sings of the "tender mercy of our God" (Lk 1:78) who "shows mercy to our ancestors" (1:72) by remembering his covenant with his mighty works which save his people from their enemies (1:71). Mary's Magnificat sings of the God who has come to the help of Israel his servant, mindful of his mercy (1:54), which extends from Abraham to his descendants for ever (1:55). The birth of John the Baptist is among God's works of mercy (*eleos*) (Lk 1:58), a merciful event in a salvation history of such events.

Jesus demands that his disciples be merciful (*oiktirmones*) "as your Father is merciful" (Lk 6:36), where the perfection of the Father is seen in the Lukan redaction of Matthew (5:48) to consist in his merciful and compassionate love for all. This is an essential condition for entering into the kingdom of heaven (Mt 5:7). Such merciful and compassionate love should make us, like the Good Samaritan (Lk 10:30-37), neighbors to the unfortunate persons we meet and forgiving towards those who have offended us (Mt 18:23-35), because God has mercifully forgiven us (Mt 18:32-33). Thus, we shall be judged according to the merciful and compassionate love that we have shown, perhaps unknowingly, to the person of Jesus (Mt 25:31-46).

The public ministry of Jesus consists in works of merciful and compassionate love for all without exception. his condemnations, admonitions, rebukes — whether towards the Pharisees or towards his own disciples — all express the merciful love of a God who would save human persons from the self-destruction that follows upon self-deception and hardness of heart. He inveighs against the Scribes and Pharisees because of his compassionate love for them. His table-fellowship with sinners manifests the same compassionate love (Lk 5:29-32). His ministry of compassion leads to his passion and death and resurrection, the culmination of his self-giving that enables Luke to write that "all flesh shall see God's salvation" (3:6). His compassion was such for all that the afflicted would address themselves to him as to God himself with their cry: "Lord, have mercy!" (Mt 15:22; 17:15; 20:30-31).

4. *The friendship of Jesus.* The goodness of Jesus towards sinners appears frequently in the Gospels, especially in *Luke*: the three parables of chapter 15, the story of the Pharisee and the publican at prayer in the Temple (18:9-14), the stories of forgiveness involving the sinful woman (7:36-50), Zaccheus (19:1-10), Peter and his denial (22:61-62), and passages which represent Jesus' calling sinners (Lk 5:32), eating with them (5:29-30), and welcoming them (15:1-2). His enemies contrast his behavior with that of John the Baptist, noting that Jesus is "a friend of tax collectors and sinners" (Lk 7:33; Mt 11:18-19). The word, friend (*philos*), occurs a second time in the Synoptic Gospels, where Jesus refers to his disciples as "my friends" (Lk 12:4). The two Lukan texts on friendship present complementary aspects

of Jesus' friendship: it is outgoing with regard to sinners and intimate with regard to the disciples with whom he lives. The outgoing love of God in Jesus Christ draws, or invites, everyone to the intimacy of communion in friendship.

Jesus gladly accepts the hospitality of others; he welcomes others. The Gospel of Luke especially emphasizes this aspect of his friendship in the episodes of the banquet of Simon the Pharisee (7:36) and two other banquets of Pharisees (11:37; 14:1). He accepts the hospitality of Martha and Mary (10:38-42); he welcomes the women who follow him in his travels and assist him and the Twelve (8:1-3). His friendship with the Twelve is a constant in all the Gospels. They share his trials and the night of his passion (Lk 22:28-29).

In sending his Son among us, God has shown himself a "friend of men" (Tt 3:4); and Jesus depicted him as one who allows himself to be influenced by an importunate friend (Lk 11:5-8). Jesus incarnates this friendship. He loved the rich young man (Mk 10:21), his friends, and even his enemies. He reveals that the love that is sovereign in God's kingdom is all-inclusive: "You have learned how it was said: you must love your neighbor and hate your enemy. But I say this to you: love your enemies" (Mt 5:43-44). Jesus appeals for the solidarity of friendship with all humankind whose goal is the kingdom of God.

II. John's Gospel

Although John speaks much of Christ's love in the passion narrative, he also describes its manifestations at length throughout his life. John had shared Jesus' public life, as he explains at the beginning of his First Letter (1 Jn 1:1-3). John calls attention to Christ's love in different contexts.

1. *Jesus' love for a family.* Jesus loved the family of Bethany: Lazarus, Martha and Mary. The sisters send a message to Jesus: "Lord, the man you love is ill'" (Jn 11:3). John affirms that Jesus loved Martha and her sister and Lazarus'" (11:5). Jesus refers to his friendship with Lazarus, associating it with both the message of the sisters and his

own disciples, who had enjoyed the family's hospitality: "Our friend Lazarus is resting, I am going to wake him" (11:11). When Jesus weeps at the death of Lazarus, the Jews say: "See how much he loved him!"(11:36). Jesus' profound compassion for his friends, and for the friends of his friends, is clear: "At the sight of her tears, and those of the Jews who followed her, Jesus said in great distress, with a sigh that came straight from the heart, "Where have you put him?" (11:34).

2. *Jesus' love for a disciple.* "The disciple Jesus loved" is first mentioned when the treachery of Judas is foretold at the Last Supper (13:27). The phrase is repeated with reference to the same person when Jesus speaks to his mother at Calvary: "Seeing his mother and the disciple he loved standing near her, Jesus said to his mother, 'Woman, this is your son'" (19:26). The third mention of this disciple occurs in the account of the events of Easter morning: "[Mary of Magdala] came running to Simon Peter and the other disciple, the one Jesus loved" (20:2). The fourth mention of the disciple occurs when Jesus makes his post-resurrectional appearance on the shore of Tiberias: "The disciple Jesus loved said to Peter, 'It is the Lord'" (21:7). The final mention of this disciple occurs after the prediction of Peter's martyrdom: "Peter turned and saw the disciple Jesus loved following them..." (21:20).

3. *Jesus' love for all the disciples.* John writes of Jesus' love for his disciples at the introduction of the account of Jesus' washing his disciples' feet (13:1). He had always loved them, "...but now he showed how perfect his love was" (13:1). He commands them to love one another (13:33-36), "'...as I have loved you'" (13:34;15:12-16). They are his friends, if they keep this commandment (15:14).

4. *Jesus' love for all future believers.* The disciples prefigure all future believers. The Father's love for Jesus is the same love that Jesus has for his disciples and all future believers. The death of Jesus is the supreme manifestation of the love which the Father communicates for the salvation of all (13:1; 15:13). The Good Shepherd gives his life for his sheep (10:15); they know one another with the fullness of knowledge that comes from intimate interpersonal relations

rooted in (the Father's) love (10:14-15). Christ has formed the flock of all those who believe in him and share his Father's love: "'I pray not only for these, but for those also who through their words will believe in me'" (17:20). The Father loves his Son (3:35; 5:19-20). The love that the Father has for his Son is the love that he has for the disciples and all human persons. His eternal love for his Son is communicated in and through his Son for the salvation of all humankind: "'If anyone loves me he will keep my word, and my Father will love him, and we shall come to him and make our home with him'" (14:23).

5. *God is love.* God's love is at the origin of all that is revealed and communicated in Jesus Christ. The eternal life hidden in the heart of God "from the beginning" has become audibly, visibly, tangibly present to the world in the advent of Jesus who was, John insists, a true human being, one whom we "touched with our hands" (1 Jn 1:1). The Christian community continues to witness this reality to the world, that those who have not seen may yet believe and receive the gift of authentic life as well. This eternal life, this authentic human existence now and forever, is life in a community of love whose vital center is the presence of the Trinity as community of love in their midst (1 Jn 1:1-4). The result of such life is complete joy: "We are writing this to you to make your joy complete" (1 Jn 1:4).

"God is Love" (1 Jn 4:8, 16); God is not a solitary person, but a community of love in dynamic interpersonal relationships. Therefore, within the community of love formed around the risen Lord and his gift of the Spirit, the ultimate sacrament of God's presence as love among us is our love for all others. To love others as Jesus Christ loved them is the external sign of vital communion with God; not to love others as Jesus Christ loved them is a sign of his absence. As God externalized his love for us in Jesus Christ and his interpersonal communications with all divine and human persons, so also we encounter the God who is Love in the sacramentality of our sharing Jesus Christ's universal love for others. That love will take as many forms as it took in the life and death of Jesus Christ.

3. JESUS DYING IN GOD'S LOVE

Introduction

The passion narratives are a theology of the history of the events surrounding the suffering and death of Jesus. Mark invites the reader to share Jesus Christ's total commitment to God in the service of all by accepting his way of the cross. Matthew calls for adoration and worship of the Lord through whose death we are reconciled with God and neighbor in the new community of Israel. Luke invites participation in the martyred Jesus' trust in God and compassion for all. And John affirms that we must celebrate the glorification of Jesus who, as the paragon of love, died that his joy in the Father might be ours. The Evangelists' portraits of Jesus' dying are not primarily history but theology with a transformational purpose. In John's words: "these things have been written in order that you may believe that Jesus is the Christ, the Son of God, and that believing you may have life in his name" (20:31).

Each Evangelist, with his particular emphasis, summons us to accept Jesus Christ and his total commitment in freedom and love to God. Each invites us to participate in the efficacy of his death for all (Mk 10:45; 14:24), for the forgiveness of sins (Mt 1:21; 26:28), in his exodus from the power of darkness (Lk 9:31; 22:53) and in his being lifted up for the life of the world (Jn 3:14; 8:28; 12:32).

The language of the Evangelists is that of a living relationship or story, of confession and conversion, of manifestation and proclamation. The Evangelists' narrative form is for our reformation or transformation, and not merely for our information. Their vision (portrait) of Jesus Christ is for the revision of our lives in Christian conversion both as event and lifelong process. The four Gospel portraits of Jesus' dying appear in four distinctive narrative forms that complement one another in fostering our commitment to God in the service of all. The particular theological orientation of each Evangelist dominates the organization of his narrative for the particular impact that Jesus' death should have on his readers.

Mark's highly *kerygmatic* account proclaims the disconcerting realization of God's design. Mark records fewer sayings and teachings but its accounts are more detailed. Mark is a Gospel of facts. His style is often that of oral improvisation-which gives his account more liveliness. Mark is not reluctant to stun us with the shocking facts; rather, he seeks to do so. His is the account of the witness who underscores contrasts and paradox: the Cross is scandalous, but it reveals the Son of God. The mystery of the Cross, in Mark, imposes itself on us and strikes us from without; it evokes an act of faith, submission to the total claims of God (15:39).

Matthew gives us an *ecclesial* and *doctrinal* account, words which clarify for an assembly of believers. Matthew presents in his great discourses a schematic and clear outline of ecclesial doctrine which befits the liturgy. He avoids the carelessness of improvisation. He is less interested than Mark in concrete detail. He insists on the fulfillment of Scripture, on the foreknowledge of Jesus, on his sovereign authority. The saving facts, the act of God in Christ, are illuminated through sharing in the faith and life of the Church.

Luke tends to make the sayings of Jesus personal. He avoids accumulating traditions in long discourses and instead he specifies the person to whom the teaching is addressed in each case. The beatitudes in Matthew have a general tone (third person), those in Luke have a direct tone (second person). Luke manifests the concerns of the historian and the writer. He tries to give a better explanation of the way in which the events unfold and to compose an account which is well-ordered. His account is that of the disciple who relieves the story of his master. Personal attachment is expressed by the repeated affirmation of the innocence of Jesus, by the omission of offensive or cruel details. For the disciple, the Passion is at the same time a call to be with Jesus on his way of the Cross. Luke's *personal* and *hortatory* account both arouses and confirms the commitment of each one for the following of Christ.

John begins his account by identifying Jesus with the pre-existent Word of God (1:1-18). John bases these verses on an early Christian hymn to Jesus as the divine Word. The reader thus knows that all he hears Jesus say and do in the course of John's narrative expresses that Word. John envisions a whole sphere of reality beyond this world, which must be revealed to be perceived. The deepest meaning of everyone and of everything in this world has its ultimate source and ground and destiny in that other world, which Jesus reveals to believers (14:8-9). God reveals himself in Jesus because he so loves the world and wills to save it (3:16-17). John uses the term "signs" for all the actions of Jesus. The incident of Cana is termed "the first of his signs" (2:11). John's account closes with the affirmation that "Jesus did many other signs in the presence of the disciples, which are not written in this book" (20:30). These "signs" show what God is and what God does. The first part of John's Gospel is called the Book of Signs (1:19—12:50). It is followed by the Book of Glory (13:1—20:31) which recounts the glorification of the Son when: "his hour had come to depart out of this world to the Father" (13:1). John's story sets forth the descent and ascent of the Word of God who is with God and is God (3:17; 4:42; 16:28). Through his cross and resurrection Jesus returns to the Father. In his words and deeds, those who believe in Jesus Christ recognize the manifestation of the Father's glory. Jesus Christ enables us to experience the impact of his way and truth and life (14:6), of his relationship with the Father becoming our own (14:9). Clement of Alexandria recognized John's as the "*spiritual*" Gospel, whose interpreter, like its author, must have "lain close to the Master's breast" (21:20) to receive "the Spirit which those who were to believe in him were to receive" (7:40). Only the Spirit, whom the Father would send in Jesus' name (14:25), can enable us to make the *intuitive* and *mystical* experience of the "beloved disciple" and author of this Gospel our own. Through the gift of the Holy Spirit, those who have not seen but yet have believed (20:29), become the true contemporaries and friends of Jesus (15:13,14,15). So advanced is the theology of this Gospel that its author has, from the earliest centuries, merited the title of "the theologian."

This survey of characteristic and distinctive emphases of the Evangelists contextualizes the four portraits of Jesus' dying without assuming that the primary concern of one author is absent in the writings of the others. On the contrary, there is an historical, theological, hortatory, and mystical concern in all the Gospels. Each is a kerygmatic story of the great deeds of God in Jesus Christ; each proclaims the good news that the life and death and resurrection of Jesus Christ is for all humankind. Each author has a theological or doctrinal concern about the true meaning and value of these events; for God has raised a question for understanding and for reflection in them. Each author has an ethical, paraenetic, hortatory, and mystical concern about these events; for God has raised a question for human decision and action with regard to our fundamental relationship with ourselves, others, the world, and God. We may know and understand the Gospel narratives; we are blessed only if we are transformed by them in our basic self-others-world-God relationship. The factual, doctrinal, ethical, and mystical concerns have their place in each Gospel. The Good News is never mere fact; it is a fact filled with an abiding divine significance for all humankind. It is never mere doctrine (religious insights, understandings, and propositional truths); it is always doctrine which illuminates a unique event both in the world outside us and within the depths of our being, which challenges all human pretensions and requires us to make a radically new beginning "as a little child," sacrificing the cherished illusion of or desire for human self-sufficiency, for the fulness of life which God alone can give and wishes to give (Jn 10:10). All the Evangelists summon us to a life of Christian mysticism: communion with God and all humankind in Jesus Christ. Through him John proclaims that we have been given the power to become the children of God (1:12).

I. Mark

The four Gospel accounts of the death of Jesus might be compared to four portraits of him. Rembrandt or Velazquez would present a rather traditional and historical likeness. El Greco presents almost translucent features and elongated limbs, a more mystical likeness. Rouault, who gives perhaps no more than a torso in bold striking colors, brings out the human suffering. Dali presents a cosmic view, the cross hovering over the world. Each presents the same story but with differing emphases; the crucifixion is, at the same time, historical, traditional, mystical, full of human suffering and cosmic.

Similarly, each Evangelist has created a portrait of the death of Jesus. We must ask why. The Evangelists were not just writing biography, nor were they concerned with the purely historical. They were writing from the resurrection faith, from which stems all the theology of the New Testament. They narrate the death of Jesus from this perspective; consequently, the meaning of his death, rather than physical detail, is their central concern.

1. TWO POINTS OF VIEW

Their Eastern view of narrative differs from our modern Western view. We must recognize this difference to grasp the purpose of the Gospel narratives.

Like the ninteenth-century German exegetes, we tend to

read the Gospel narratives with a primarily historical interest in *what actually* happened. The Evangelists and their Christian contemporaries, however, were more interested in the theological meaning of these facts. Their question is not so much "What took place?" but rather "What was going on in what took place?" Although history is important, the primary concern of the Evangelists is not that of providing historical information. They make no attempt to bring out the physical aspects of Jesus' death; rather they underscore its significance. Blood, for example, is not mentioned in the Synoptics' descriptions of his death, even though the blood of the Eucharist is proposed as drink (Mk 14:23ff; Mt 26:27-29; Lk 22:20; Jn 6:53-55; 1 Cor 11:25-27).

The Evangelists employed the Old Testament to bring out the meaning of Jesus' giving his life in freedom and love for all. The Old Testament provides the context for grasping the sacramental significance of the paschal mystery of Jesus' giving up his life for the resurrection of all. Leviticus 17:10-16 and Deuteronomy 12:23 tell us that the life of any creature is in the blood, the *nephesh*, the flesh, the life-principle. God forbade the Israelites to drink it because he alone was to be their life-principle, their Lord. When the Evangelists speak of Jesus' blood poured out, they are not speaking of just his physical blood, but of his life given for us. Of primary theological interest is the meaning of the blood that is shed historically. When we are asked to drink of his blood we are asked to accept his life as our own.

2. SERVANT OF GOD FOR ALL

In Mark's view Jesus is the Servant of God. His theological perspective in Mk 10:45, "'The Son of Man came not to be served, but to serve and to give his life as a ransom for many'", is summarized by the words 'for many' (*anti pollon*). And in Mk 14:24, "'This is my blood, the blood of the Covenant, which is to be poured out for many'" (*huper pollon*), he makes the same point. These phrases, 'for many', are not used elsewhere in the New Testament save in parallel texts by Matthew which directly depend on Mk (Mt 20:28

anti pollon and Mt 26:28 *peri pollon*). In the context of Semitic languages (Aramaic and Hebrew) the word 'many' (*rabbîm*) is not exclusive: it does not leave anyone out. It is equivalent to the English word 'all'. Mark has preserved an ancient formula, more primitive than the Greek *pantôn* ("all") of 1 Timothy 2:6, which he attributes to Jesus and uses for his theological interpretation of the purpose of Jesus' death. Jesus dies 'for many', without excluding anyone, or 'for all'. This is not a uniquely Marcan view. The Church has always affirmed the universal purpose of Christ's saving death. Since Mark was the first Evangelist to record this phrase and since he preserves what is probably the oldest expression of it, we can characterize his interpretation of the theology of the death of Jesus by his words 'for many'. This expression, and its New Testament variants 'for you', 'for sinners', 'for the just', mean that the death of Jesus has an efficacy which communicates life for all, in every place and time.

3. THE EIGHT LAST MOMENTS

How does Mark's theological narrative describe this unique death? "It was the third hour when they crucified him" (15:25); "From the sixth hour there was darkness over the whole land, until the ninth hour" (15:33). In these texts there are two important elements: the duration of the crucifixion and the duration of the darkness. Mark divides the last day of Jesus' life into eight periods of three hours each, in each of which an important event is recorded.[1] For the Jews the day begins at sunset and ends at the following sunset, and in Roman times there were twelve daytime

---

[1] MARK'S TIMETABLE FOR THE LAST DAY, THE PASSOVER, OF JESUS

Text time	Modern time	Reference	Event
(Thursday)			
evening (after sunset)	1800	14:17	Passover Meal of Jesus and the Twelve. Prediction about Judas.
night	2100	14:30	Prediction about Peter, Gethsemane.

hours from sunrise to sunset, and four night watches of three hours each.

Starting with the Last Supper, Mark begins the Day of Passion at sunset. After their Passover meal, Jesus and his disciples leave for Gethsemane. Mark tells us that it is 'night', or about 9:00 p.m. Jesus prays for an hour: "'Could you not watch one hour with me?'" (14:37); and then two more hours until midnight when he is arrested and taken to the high priests. Then we read that Peter continued denying him until the cock crew for the second time, or about 3:00 a.m. (The "second cock crew" was a Roman technical term for the last of the four night watches, it was about 3:00 a.m.; see Mark 13:35.) The trial of Jesus begins at sunrise (about 6:00 a.m.). He is crucified at the third hour (9:00 a.m.). At

(Friday)			
after 3 hours	2400	14:37-41	Arrest of Jesus, Interrogation begins.
(first cockcrow)		14:68	Peter's first denial.
second cockcrow	300	14:72	Peter's last denials.
early morning	600	15:1	Trial before Pilate.
			Temple Gates open for beginning of worship. Recitation of the *Shema*, "Hear, O Israel!"
third hour	900	15:25	Crucifixion
			The first lambs are sacrificed in the Temple.
sixth hour	1200	15:33	Darkness begins (recalling the ninth plague and prophecies of the Last Day by Amos, Jeremiah, and Joel).
ninth hour	1500	15:34-37	Darkness ends after 3 hours (3 days in Exodus).
			Death of Jesus (recalling the tenth plague) after his loud cry (recalling Joel's prophecy of the Last Day, i.e. 15:37).
			Trumpets call faithful to Temple for the sacrifice of the last lamb.
			Passover Feast ends when the last participant falls asleep.
evening	1800	15:42	The burial of Jesus.
(before sunset)			The Temple Gates are closed with the conclusion of worship, which occurs only in the 12 daylight hours and never in the darkness.
			The Jewish day concludes at sundown.
			The *Shema* to be recited (Dt 6:7 "... when you lie down, and when you rise").

the sixth hour the darkness begins, about 12 noon, and at the ninth hour, immediately after the darkness ends, Jesus cries out and dies, about 3:00 p.m. He stays on the cross until sunset (6:00 p.m.) when he is taken down and buried. In other words, Jesus has been hanging on the cross for nine hours (9:00 a.m. to 6:00 p.m.), six of those still alive. We must ask why Mark alone provides this chronological information.

Mark employs this artificial time schedule for a particular purpose, which seems to be related to a liturgical or catechetical structure in the early Church.[2] It probably corresponds to the way that the Church in Mark's day celebrated the important events of the Passion. Every three hours the Christian community would commemorate and teach the meaning of a particular event. Early Christians took this schedule for liturgical prayer from the Jews.

4. THE BLOOD OF THE LAMB

Daily, pious Jews recited the *shema*, the prayer taken from Deuteronomy 6:4 "Hear, O Israel, the Lord your God is one God...", at sunrise and at sunset. They also prayed the psalms of praise at the same hours and at the ninth hour (3:00 p.m.). At the time of Christ, lambs were sacrificed twice daily in the Temple, at the third (9:00 a.m.) and at the ninth (3:00 p.m.) hour. Mark tells us that Jesus, the real lamb that is sacrificed for all, was crucified when the first lambs were sacrificed in the morning (9:00 a.m.) and died when the last lambs were sacrificed in the afternoon (3:00 p.m.). These are also the times when trumpets would sound from the Temple calling the faithful to worship God in his holy sanctuary.

The gates of the Temple were opened at sunrise and closed at sunset, which correspond respectively, in Mark's

---

[2] It is similar to his parable on watching (Mk 13:33-37) and Matthew's of the landowner going out into the market square every three hours to hire laborers (Mt 20:1-16).

narrative, to the times at which Jesus is sentenced to death and is buried.

Mark implies the saving power of Jesus' death by linking it temporarily with the sacrifice of the lambs in the Temple. Mark evokes the blood-of-the-lamb symbolism of the original Passover event to communicate his theological interpretation of Jesus' death. The blood of the lambs was sprinkled on the door posts (Ex 12:13) to save the first-born sons of the Hebrews from death during the tenth plague that struck the Egyptians. Thus Mark uses the times of the Temple sacrifices to recall the time of the first Passover sacrifice. All these times, for Mark, reflect the meaning of the end-time event that is God's saving act of judgment in the death of Jesus, the real lamb.

The times for liturgical prayer in the Temple become those for prayer in the Christian community. The *hours* of the Christian breviary still correspond to the times of prayer in the Jewish liturgy.

5. THREE HOURS OF DARKNESS

Mark employs the symbol of darkness, which lasts for three hours, to interpret the meaning of Jesus' death: "At the sixth hour there was darkness over the whole land until the ninth hour" (15:23). If ours is a purely historical interest, we shall miss the theological significance of Mark's narrative. Early twentieth-century commentators asked whether the darkness referred to an eclipse, a desert sandstorm, or to some other meteorological phenomenon. There is no specific answer at this level, and neither need there be; for Mark is not making a weather report. Does the darkness represent a portent or a prodigy? Again, apart from there being no similar example in other ancient literature, this is not Mark's interest.

6. DARKNESS OVERCOME

The word that Mark uses for darkness, *skòtos*, is nowhere employed in the New Testament in a purely physical sense, but always in a figurative or metaphorical sense: there are those who walk or sit in darkness, who are cast into the outer darkness. Darkness also has an eschatological sense: the final day of the Lord is one of darkness. In these cases, the darkness represents the state of alienation, or separation, from God. This symbolic meaning of Darkness helps us to understand why Mark repeats that "at the ninth hour" (15:33, 34) only when the darkness is over, does Jesus utter his prayer from the cross: "'My God, my God, why have you abandoned me?'" (15:34 = Ps 21 [22]:1). Jesus cries out in a loud voice *after* the darkness because Mark is telling us that through his death God has finally terminated the state of alienation or separation between Himself and humankind. His voice is heard to utter a traditional prayer of Israel's Temple liturgy.

Mark is telling us that God has come in a final act of saving judgment to overcome everything that the darkness had traditionally symbolized in the relationship between God and humankind. Mark underscores the meaning of Jesus as the new Temple by having him utter a psalm of Israel's traditional Temple worship *after* the three hour period of darkness. The Jewish Temple liturgy took place in the light of day, not at night, in the hours of darkness! The darkness at midday is an obvious Marcan reference to eschatological sayings of Israel's prophets concerning God's final act of saving judgment (see Amos 8:9; Jer 15:9; Joel 3:16). God achieves his final victory over all that the darkness represents through the suffering and dying and rising of Jesus.

7. PASSOVER SYMBOLISM

Three elements are especially helpful for grasping the theological meaning of Mark's Passover symbolism of darkness: (1) no mention of the sun; (2) a three-hour period of darkness; (3) the darkness occurs before Jesus' death.

Because Jesus dies at the time of the Jewish Passover, Mark appropriately employs Passover symbolism in his theological narrative. The darkness recalls the ninth plague which punished the Egyptians and brought nearer the liberation of the Hebrews: "The Lord said to Moses 'Stretch out your hand toward heaven that there may be a darkness over all the land of Egypt, a darkness to be felt'. So Moses stretched out his hand toward heaven and there was thick darkness over all the land of Egypt for three days" (Ex 10:21-23). There are three elements of darkness in the Exodus Passover symbolism: (1) no mention of the sun; (2) it lasts for three days; (3) it is followed by the tenth plague, the death of the first-born Egyptian males (Ex 11:5).

Mark clearly evokes the saving Exodus event of divine judgment by using the same three elements in his darkness symbolism: (1) no mention of the sun; (2) it lasts for three hours; (3) it is immediately followed by the death of the first-born and beloved Son of God. (Mark parallels this with the parable of the wicked husbandmen who kill the beloved and only son, 12:1-11). Through his use of parallelism, Mark implies that just as the death of the first-born sons of the Egyptians is a divine judgment for the liberation of the Hebrews from the bondage of Egypt, so too the death of the first-born and beloved Son of God is the divine judgment for the salvation/liberation of all humankind. (God's judgment in the tenth plague has a negative note of vengeance in it as a reprisal for the Egyptian slaughter of the Hebrew male children, from which Moses was spared, Ex 1:16). The death of Jesus, on the other hand, is a divine judgment for the salvation of all.

8. PLAGUE SYMBOLISM

Mark employs the biblical sign value of the plague as an act of divine judgment. These acts can have both a negative and a positive aspect. One may be judged guilty or innocent; one may be condemned or saved. The condemnation of the guilty may also be for the salvation of the innocent. God's judgment is one of condemnation of the Egyptians in the tenth plague for their having killed the sons of the Hebrews (Ex 1:16). His acts of judgment in all ten plagues are for the liberation of the Hebrews (Ex 6:6; 7:4). All these great acts of judgment are described as signs which God performs, "to let you know that I am Yahweh" (Ex 10:2). For the Hebrews, God reveals himself most clearly in what he *does*.

Jesus' death, in Mark's narrative, is such a sign of saving judgment to let all know that he is the Son of God. Mark's literary symbolism implies that we must interpret Jesus' death in terms of the deepest meaning of the Exodus event of which it is the ultimate fulfillment. This event is the basis of both Old and New Testament theologizing. In answer to the question "Who is Yahweh, God?" the Jews would not answer "The Supreme Being" or "The Ultimate Reality"; rather they would answer: "He is the One who brought us out of the land of Egypt into the Promised land". They knew their God concretely in their experience of His great act of saving judgment. Similarly, Mark is the spokesman for the community of Christians who know their God as the Father of Jesus Christ, the Son of God, in their experience of His great act of saving judgment in the death of Jesus. Mark employs the symbolism of God's saving judgment in the original passover, or Exodus, event to express the meaning of His judgment in the death of Jesus.

9. "CRYING OUT IN A LOUD VOICE"

After the darkness ends, Jesus utters his last words, crying out with a loud voice: "'My God, my God why have you abandoned me?'" (15:34). These words are extraordinary on two counts. It is the only time in the New Testament that Jesus prays without invoking God as Father and quotes Scripture (Ps 21 [22]:1) in his prayers, even though he frequently quotes Scripture elsewhere.

What does Mark want us to understand by the final words that he ascribes to Jesus? Doubtless, they express extreme suffering and anguish, feelings of utter desolation and dereliction; but still his prayer from Scripture implies that he is at one with the will of his Father before death. Were these words of despair, they could have hardly engendered the confession of faith of the centurion who witnessed the way he died! His dying, in both *word* and deed, leads the centurion to confess that Jesus is the Son of God! God has not chosen to let this "hour" pass nor has he chosen to remove this cup (see 14:35-36); rather, God allows Jesus to be delivered into the hands of his enemies. Paul affirms (Rom 8:32) that God delivered up his own Son for us all, and Peter (1 Pt 3:18) says that this was the "Just One" dying for the "unjust ones". Mark expresses in Jesus' last words the suffering of the Just One, the sufferer in Pss 21 (22) and 68 (69), who fully experiences what it means to be delivered up by God for the salvation of all. Jesus willingly accepts this suffering as the servant of God in the service of all. His intense pain of utter abandonment expresses the price that he has willingly paid in self-abandonment to his Father's will for the salvation of all. Mark's theology is that of the early Christian tradition which affirms that Jesus willingly has been "delivered up" both by himself (Eph 5:2, 25) and by the Father (Rom 8:32). He is willingly the servant of God. He fully entrusts himself to God in his service on behalf of all, recalling the Servant of God in Isaiah who was delivered up for our salvation (Is 52 and 53).

10. PSALM OF THE JUST ONE

The psalm which Jesus utters expresses the suffering and the hope of the just man in his total commitment to God. It is the prayer of the Temple liturgy which is now uttered by the true Lamb at the moment of his free and complete self-sacrifice or self-giving for all. The blood of the Lamb is poured out to become the life-principle for all. Jesus achieves God's salvation for all, dying with a prayer on his lips that excludes any question of despair. The signs that follow his prayer indicate that he has not been abandoned. His prayer is that of the just, innocent, faithful Servant of God. Mark implies that his is a service which he alone can perform by portraying Jesus dying alone with none of his friends near him. With dramatic irony, at the moment that Jesus gives his life for all, he is apparently abandoned by all.

The last words of Jesus express Mark's theological commentary on his death. Mark intends us to recall the entire psalm. Reciting the first verse of a psalm in the Temple liturgy and in the Passover rites was an invitation to join in the recitation of the entire psalm. Mark intends us to understand that the meaning of the psalm as a whole is fulfilled in Jesus. The great eschatological triumph of God in Jesus is, for Mark, the ultimate meaning or fulfillment of the sense of triumph expressed by the suffering just man of the psalm. Jesus invites all to share the prayer that expresses his lifelong commitment to his Father. He leads the people of God to prayerful communion with the Father. The entire life of Jesus is understood as one continuous prayer which he invites all to make their own.

11. THE TORN VEIL

Between the account of Jesus' death (15:37) and the confession made by the centurion upon witnessing Jesus' death (15:39), Mark reports the rending of the Temple veil (15:38). Mark employs the rending of the Temple veil, no less than Psalm 21 (22), to interpret the meaning of the cross. With the rending of the Temple veil, the theme of Jesus replacing the Temple as the true locus of the divine presence is completed. The author of Hebrews understands this tradition in the same way when he interprets the story in terms of the Christian worship of Jesus Christ in whom we have direct access to the true Holy of Holies, the presence of God himself (Heb 10:19-20). In Mark's mind, the death of Jesus is a divine judgment. The God whose "face" or "presence" was veiled within the "Holy of Holies" (Ex 33:11, 14) himself rips away the veil and shows his "face" and manifests his "presence" in Jesus Christ, the Son of God. Mark draws out metaphorically the self-revelatory force and self-communicating efficacy of God's act of saving judgment in the self-oblation of Jesus. Through his death, which culminates his mission of suffering and service, Jesus' true identity is manifested; and the effect, according to Mark, is that of God himself showing his "face" in that of the Son of God, recognized as such by the centurion. Mark employs symbols of Jewish Temple worship, the psalm and the Temple veil, to express the meaning of Jesus and his death. Mark, thus, resolves the two chief preoccupations of his narrative: (1) Jesus' rejection and suffering, which culminates with his death (15:37) and (2) the revelation and recognition of Jesus' identity, which culminates with the centurion's confession (15:39). On the presupposition that these two preoccupations may be viewed as the central driving forces of Mark's narrative, the literary and theological symbolism of the torn veil is of major significance; for we assume that the Gospel is a literary-theological whole. The interpretation of a particular passage turns primarily on our examination of the way that it functions in the structure of the whole, the way it picks up or develops the motifs and themes that characterize the remainder of the Gospel, the way it makes use of distinctive words, phrases, appellations, actions and characters.

12. THE TEMPLE MOTIF

Mark forges a theological interpretation of Jesus' death in terms of symbols central to Jewish worship. The theme of Jesus' death is closely interwoven with the Temple motif from the moment of his entry into Jerusalem where his Passion will be consummated (10:32-34). Jesus cleanses the Temple (11:15-19). He scorns those who keep it (12:12-27, 38-40). He predicts its ultimate destruction (13:1-2). The two charges at his trial (14:58, 61), the twofold mockery beneath the cross (15:29, 32), and the two reported consequences of his death (15:38, 39) evidence the vital connection between Mark's christological interests and his literary-theological use of the Temple motif to affirm that Jesus is the suffering Servant of God who will build the eschatological temple "not made with hands" (14:58). Temple destruction and rebuilding is a Markan metaphor for Jesus' rejection (14:58), suffering (15:29), death (15:38), and resurrection. The crucified and risen Christ is, for Mark, the true Temple, the true center of the divine presence and worship; consequently, right worship for all humankind is redefined as taking up the cross and following him in total commitment to God in the service of all.

13. A NEW MEANING FOR THE SACRED

Mark reinterprets the traditional Jewish notion of the sacred through his use of the Temple motif. The radicalness of this reinterpretation is the motive for having Jesus condemned to death. That Jesus becomes in himself the Temple's replacement is the point of the accusation at his trial: "'We heard him say "I am going to destroy this Temple made by human hands and in three days build another, not made by human hands"' (14:58). The holiness of the Temple was linked with the notion of separateness, based on the belief that God is the most holy and the most separate. The holiness of his dwelling place, the Temple, therefore required separateness. Similarly the holiness of the Holy Land and the Holy City separated them, respectively, from all other lands and cities. Even the Temple, a huge edifice covering a fifth of the whole area of Jerusalem, was constructed and divided into many sections on the basis of the degrees of separateness between God and humankind. The Gentiles could enter the outer court of the Temple, because they too were creatures of God. However, since they did not follow the law, they were not as holy as the Jews who could enter into the inner court, a more holy and separate place. Jewish men, as opposed to women, could go one stage further to the court of Israel beyond which only priests could go, to the Holy Place, the Temple proper. (Jesus, a layman, could not enter this section. He was not a Jewish priest of Israel; his priesthood stems from his death and resurrection. The letter to the Hebrews describes his as a different priesthood according to the order of Melchizedek.) And in their turn, only one priest at a time could approach the Holy of Holies to offer incense (Lk 1:9).

Physical barriers, walls, doors and the veil, represented the stages of holiness in the Temple. The Holy of Holies was inside the priests' court, screened off by the great Temple veil, behind which God dwelt in glory and were kept the holiest treasures of Judaism: the Ark of the Covenant, the manna from the desert, the staff of Aaron (1 Kgs 8:6). Although all these disappeared at the time of the destruction of the Temple and the exile (2 Ch 36:18), the Holy of Holies, in the rebuilt Temple, was still considered to be as holy as ever. This inner sanctuary was entered only once a year, at *Yom Kippur*, by the High Priest (1 Kgs 8:10) who filled the place with incense to maintain the separation between himself and God.

14. BREAKING THE BARRIERS

All these barriers show us just how electrifying Mark's statement is that at the death of Jesus the Temple veil of separation was torn asunder. Through the symbolism of the torn veil, Mark tells us that God has performed an act of destructive and saving judgment. Through the self-oblation of Jesus Christ, the Son of God, at Golgotha God has destroyed all the barriers and separations between Himself and humankind; He has also created a direct access to Himself for all humankind in Jesus Christ, His Son, the Beloved (1:11; 9:7).

15. "I AM"

Mark employs a series of 'I am' (*ego eimi*) statements in which Jesus identifies himself in the same way that God identifies Himself to Moses in the theophany at the burning bush (Ex 3:6). Only God and his divine Son can say 'I am' with authority. Jesus warns his disciples that others will attempt to arrogate this divine title to themselves (13:5-6). There are only two other times that Jesus identifies himself with this title in Mark's narrative: whilst walking on the sea (6:50) and before the High Priest (14:62).

16. A HOUSE FOR ALL NATIONS

There is evidence that the Messiah will destroy his enemies, will conquer evil by the breath of his mouth (confer Is 11:4; 4 Ezra 13:4; Ethiopian Enoch 62:2). This evidence may help to explain the curious description which Mark gives of Jesus' death. A crucified man would be so weak that he would die with hardly a groan, let alone a loud cry: "And Jesus uttered a loud cry, and breathed his last." And the veil of the Temple was torn in two, from top to bottom. And when the centurion, who stood facing him, saw that he thus *breathed his last*, he said, 'Truly, this man was the Son of God!'" (15:37-39). The centurion's confession of Jesus as the Son of God makes clear that Jesus' death provides entry for all into the sanctuary: all can draw near to God through and in the Son of God. The Temple veil no longer hides God's glory. This glory is seen in the crucified, who has established a new people in fulfillment of the prophecy: "'My house shall be called a house of prayer *for all the nations*'" (11:17). He has poured out his life for all (14:24), the life which forms the new Temple and its people.

To ask whether the Temple veil was really torn asunder would be to miss Mark's point. The torn veil symbolizes the end of the old covenant and the beginning of the new. A new ritual and cult and Temple replace the old. The meaning of the new beginning is linked to Mark's word for describing the rending of the veil (*eschìsthê* = "was rent"). The only other place where Mark uses the verb is in recounting the baptism of Jesus: "... he saw the heavens being rent (*schizoménous*) and the Spirit, like a dove, descending on him" (1:10). The heavens are envisioned as a cloth or veil torn asunder to allow the Spirit to descend and the "voice from heaven" to be experienced or heard affirming," 'You are my Son, the Beloved'" (1:11). Jesus' mission as the Servant of God originates in his experience and possession of the Spirit of God. His mission is completed by his communication of this same Spirit that will enable all others to share his life, poured out for all (14:24), and to hear that same voice which identifies him as the Beloved Son of God. His God-given mission and service for all is to communicate the loving presence of the Spirit, that all might fully share his life as beloved children of God.

17. THE CENTURION: VOICE OF FAITH

Thus, Mark's story closes as it opened with the words acclaiming Jesus as the Son of God. God's announcement of Jesus as his Son in the voice from heaven (1:11) is acknowledged, significantly, by a gentile Roman centurion (15:39), the first human person in Mark's narrative to make the full Christian confession of faith: Jesus is the Son of God. That the first Christian confession of faith should come from a gentile symbolizes the efficacy and universal scope of the Servant who gives his life for all. He represents all who make the same Christian confession of faith in Jesus Christ through the power of the Spirit of God which his total commitment to God at Golgotha has revealed and communicated. Mark is interested in the individual gentile centurion only as representing all those who are saved by the death of Jesus and his communicating the Spirit of God. For Mark he is the spokesman for the Christian faith and for the Gentiles who are called by God to join the Jews as the people of God. To ask whether an individual Roman centurion had historically made such a full affirmation of Christian faith would be to miss the point. Only through the death of Jesus can anyone acknowledge that he is the Son of God.

Mark implies that only through the gift of the Spirit of God can anyone fully recognize and accept the Son of God. In the account of Jesus' baptism, Mark links Jesus' possession of the Spirit of God with his self-knowledge, vocation and mission as the Son of God, the Beloved. The divine voice that Jesus hears at his baptism, which inaugurates his mission as the Servant of God (1:11), quotes from the coronation Psalm (Ps 2:7) which Mark intends as an announcement of who Jesus is and how he will function as God's obedient Son, to which the centurion's affirmation is the appropriate response. Mark also quotes from Deutero-Isaiah's reference to his ordination as a prophet (Is 42:1). God has given his Servant his Spirit that he might bring his righteousness to all. Mark relates that Jesus *"breathed his last"* (15:36) with the implication that he has completed his God-given mission with his communication of the Spirit of God that had inaugurated it. If we recall that the root meaning of 'spirit' is 'breath' and by extension the life principle of the living, then Mark's Gentile centurion would represent all those who have accepted the Spirit of God as the new life principle which Jesus has 'breathed' into them in his total self-commitment on Golgotha. Only those who have accepted the Spirit as their own life principle can truly recognize and confess Jesus Christ to be the Son of God. In recounting Jesus' constant repudiation of the apparently true confessions of demons and demoniacs, Mark might well be implying that Christians who confess Jesus with their tongues but have no love for him in their hearts, devoid of the Spirit of God, are really no different from the devils in their meaningless affirmations that he is their Lord, their Beloved, the Son of their God!

18. MISSION COMPLETED

The High Priest's circumlocution for the Godhead ('Son of the Blessed') and the charge of blasphemy (cf. 2:7) both indicate that Mark considers Jesus' divinity to be the real bone of contention at his trial. At the very beginning of the narrative, Jesus is identified as the "Christ, Son of God" (1:1). At the two Christophanic episodes of the baptism (1:11) and the Transfiguration (9:7), the voice of God is heard identifying Jesus as "'My Son, the Beloved'". Mark balances the baptismal scene (in which Jesus alone hears that voice) with the scene at Golgotha. Jesus' mission, as Servant of God, is inaugurated at his baptism and completed through his filial self-surrender to God on the cross when the centurion declares that Jesus is "the Son of God". Both the heavens rent at the baptism and the Temple veil rent at the death of Jesus allow direct communication with God for the true identification of Jesus as Christ, Son of God, the Beloved. Mark underscores the link between these two scenes with the Transfiguration episode which occurs six days after Jesus' first formal announcement of his coming passion and death (8:31; 9:2-7), when the voice of God is again heard identifying Jesus as "'My Son, the Beloved'" (9:7). The centurion's confession that Jesus is "'the Son of God'" parallels the voice of God at the baptism and the Transfiguration. Mark makes the centurion the symbol of all who make the full Christian confession of belief in the divine sonship of Jesus and benefit from the saving effect of God's judgment.

19. THE CROSS REVEALS

The torn veil and the centurion's confession are the two signs following Jesus' death that contextualize the meaning of Jesus' shout "My God, my God, why have you abandoned me?" God did not, indeed, abandon his Son who was on the cross in fulfillment of his Father's will for the salvation of all humankind. Jesus final prayer expresses both the cost and the incomparable benefits of total self-abandonment to God. Nothing in all creation, not even death itself, separates the Son of God, the Beloved, from his Father. His final prayer brings to completion his prayer at Gethsemane: "'Not my will, but thine be done'" (14:36). In the apocalyptic language of Psalm 21(22) Jesus expresses an entire life and death based on the absolute trustworthiness of God and utter confidence in the coming of His kingdom.

For Mark the cross is the chief locus of revelation. There, Jesus gives himself totally to the Father in freedom and love. The Father is the Supreme Good of all. Thus, the cross is the place where Jesus Christ fulfills his service for all humankind. It is the place where he is recognized as the Son of God; and it is in a similar way that his disciples will be known.

II. Matthew

1. "FOR THE FORGIVENESS OF SINS"

In Matthew "Jesus" is not simply a name, but a title — he who "will save his people from their sins" (1:21). In contrast to Mark, Matthew introduces the major parts of his passion narrative with the title "Jesus", the key to his interpretation of the death in which Jesus accomplishes his life-mission. For Matthew, the forgiveness of sins is achieved only through the death of Jesus; consequently, even though he generally follows Mark closely, he omits Mark's reference to John's baptism of repentance "'for the forgiveness of sins'" (Mk 1:4 = Lk 3:3) and adds to Mark's words of Jesus over the cup at the Last Supper that his blood is to be poured out for many "for the forgiveness of sins (Mk 14:24 = Mt 26:28). Although both affirm that Jesus pours out his life for all, Matthew emphasizes that Jesus' death overcomes the obstacle that sin is to the reception of his life. His teaching recalls that of earlier New Testament writings (1 Cor 15:3; Eph 1:7; Col 1:14, and Heb 9:22); however, his expression in Jesus' words over the cup is unique among the Gospel accounts. His theological interpretation of Jesus' death is distinguished by the words "for the forgiveness of sins".

2. ESCHATOLOGICAL SIGNS: JOEL

The Synoptic writers employ eschatological signs from the prophet Joel to bring out the meaning of Jesus' death. Joel's contribution was to prophesy in an apocalyptic poem the outpouring of the Spirit on all God's people in the messianic age (Joel 3:1-2), portents of the day of Yahweh (Joel 3:3-5), the judgement of the nations in the valley of Jehoshaphat (Joel 4:1-8, 9-14), and the deliverance of Israel (Joel 4:10-21).

Mark, stressing the Suffering Servant's pain of self-abandonment to the total demands of God for the ransom of all (Mk 15:34), narrates that Jesus died with *a loud cry* after *darkness* (also Amos 8:9) had covered the land, employing two signs of God's judgment, according to Joel 4:15-16. Matthew adds further signs from Joel (27:45, 51-53) to underscore the eschatological significance of Jesus' death. Besides the darkness and the voice of Yahweh that roars from Jerusalem (Zion), Matthew tells of the earthquake, recalling Joel's description of the day of Yahweh (Joel 4:16). He evokes Joel's prophecy of the outpouring of the Spirit in the description of Jesus' death, which introduces the eschatological turning point of the ages: "But Jesus, again crying out in a loud voice, yielded up (*aphêken* = let go) his spirit" (27:50).

3. ESCHATOLOGICAL SIGNS: EZECHIEL

Immediately after the death of Jesus, the veil of the Temple was torn from top to bottom; the earth quaked; the rocks were split. Then, Matthew relates that "the tombs opened and the bodies of many saints rose from the dead, and these, after his resurrection came out of the tombs, entered the Holy City and appeared to a number of people" (27:52-53). Matthew seems to be employing the imagery of Ezechiel's dry-bones prophecy to affirm the deepest meaning if Jesus' death:

> "So prophesy. Say to them, 'The Lord Yahweh says this: I am now going to open your graves; I mean to raise you from your graves, my people, and lead you back to the soil of Israel. And you will know that I am Yahweh, when I open your graves and raise you from your graves, my people. And I shall put my Spirit in you, and you will live, and I shall resettle you on your own soil; and you will know that I, Yahweh, have said and done this — it is the Lord Yahweh who speaks" (Ez 37:12-14).

Jesus' death and resurrection, for Matthew, are distinct

aspects of one event. The resurrection begins at the death of Jesus. The resurrected just represent the impact and meaning of the event. The holy ones of Israel are even now rising through the yielding up of Jesus' spirit. The final resurrection of all the just has even now begun in its "first fruit" (cf. 1 Cor 15:20). Israel's hopes, expressed in Ezechiel's prophecy, are being fulfilled through the spirit of God that Jesus is communicating for the rising of the just. God is putting his spirit in his people for a rebirth that will enable them to "know God" in the full biblical sense.

4. THE FIRST TO BENEFIT

Matthew uses the word "saints", or "holy ones", only once in his entire Gospel (27:52). What is most extraordinary is his application of the word. Throughout the New Testament "saints" or "holy ones" invariably refers to Christians, *living* Christians. Matthew takes a word that has applied only to Christians and applies it to the Jews of the Old Testament to underscore that Jesus' death is for the forgiveness of all, Jews and Gentiles.

Although the Gentiles, represented by the Magi (2:1-12), are the first to visit Jesus, the Jews, represented by the resurrected dead, are the first to benefit from Jesus' yielding up his spirit. Earlier in his Gospel, Matthew alludes to the faithful Jews who had hoped in God's promises and awaited his Messiah: "'For truly I say to you many prophets and righteous men desired to see, and did not, to hear, and did not, these things that you see and hear'" (13:17). The saints of Israel are the first beneficiaries of Jesus' death for the forgiveness of all. Jesus had willingly accepted death for the forgiveness and rebirth of his own people. (That he had willingly given up his life is underscored by Matthew's reference to the more than twelve legions of angels at Jesus' disposal were he to have asked for them: 26:52-54).

The importance of Matthew's reference to the saints of the old covenant becomes clear when we advert to the fact that he has placed this sign (linked with the earthquake) immeidately after the rending of the Temple veil. Both Mark and Matthew regard the torn veil as symbolic of the end of the old covenant. For both, however, it is more than a negative symbol. Mark relates it immediately to the centurion's confession of the new faith. Matthew, however, seeks to balance the negative symbolism related to the old covenant with positive symbolism related to that covenant. He accomplishes this by showing that at the death of Jesus God raised up from the dead ones the just of Israel. He gives them the same name and status as new covenant "saints". Israel's saints had confessed the one and true God through whose redemptive power the just of both covenants shall rise. Matthew affirms that Jesus came to fulfill the Law and the prophets. Through his death the old covenant has attained its completion (see 5:17). The holiness and righteousness of those who had faithfully observed the old covenant ultimately derives from Jesus, the Servant whom God has appointed as a covenant of the people for all nations (Is 42:6).

If the resurrection of Israel's saints is the result of and absolutely dependent on the death of Jesus, then he is clearly the first of those whom God has raised from the dead. The time factor is irrelevant for Matthew, whose main concern is to affirm that the resurrection of the saints depends entirely upon Jesus' yielding up his spirit for all. He does, however, relate the appearances of the resurrected saints to a definite time factor. They are not made visible until after Jesus' own resurrection when they went into the Holy City (27:53). (Matthew had referred to the "Holy City" in the scene where the Devil takes Jesus to the pinnacle of the Temple in Jerusalem: 4:5.) The appearance of the resurrected saints in the Holy City recalls the passage in Daniel (Dan 12:2), which shows the eschatological character of the resurrection of the dead. It also seems to be related to the eschatological signs (darkness, shout, earthquake) that Joel (Joel 4:14-17) relates to the day of Yahweh. After these signs, God will be a refuge for his people and they will know that he dwells in Zion his holy mountain, "'and Jerusalem shall be holy'" (Joel 4:17).

5. CONFESSION OF FAITH

The centurion's confession in Matthew, as in Mark, is a positive sign of God's saving judgment that follows the eschatological darkness and loud shout. In Matthew's narrative, however, the confession follows the resurrection of the old covenant saints and thereby takes on a new meaning. In Matthew's account it is not the manner of Jesus' death alone that motivates the centurion's confession but rather the earthquake and accompanying events (27:54). These events do not include the torn veil and the resurrected dead, for neither occurs on Golgotha. The saints appear only after Jesus' resurrection. Matthew presents the earthquake as a truly historical event and not merely an eschatological sign. As such, it engenders the fear among the soldiers and apparently moves them to make their confession of faith. In contrast with Mark, where the centurion alone makes the confession of faith, Matthew has both the centurion and the accompanying soldiers make a choral declaration of faith. Matthew balances two groups to show the efficacy of Jesus' death: the Israelite saints representing the people of the old covenant and the Gentile soldiers representing those of the new covenant. Jesus' death achieves the forgiveness of sins for all (26:28).

Matthew, like Mark, intends the soldiers' affirmation to be understood as a full Christian confession of faith in Jesus as the Son of God. Their words are almost the same as those that Matthew has in his account of the disciples, who as a group had witnessed Jesus walking on the sea: "'Truly you are the Son of God'" (14:33). Jesus' unique sonship is affirmed, although in neither case is the article employed.

In Mark, the only human to call Jesus "the Son of God" is the centurion. This is not the case in Matthew's narrative. Both the disciples (14:33) and Simon Peter (16:16) confess that Jesus is the Son of God. At the religious trial, Jesus is asked if he is the Son of God (26:63), and at Golgotha he is twice mocked as the Son of God (27:40, 43).

6. JESUS: THE QUESTION

The Gospel writers give their theological narrative a form for transforming and reforming human life. The form is for our performance. The questions that pervade Gospel narratives are for our understanding and reflection and performance. Our affirming that "Jesus is the answer" must be balanced with our recognizing that Jesus is no less the question that God has raised about the true goodness and direction of our lives. The Gospel writers want their readers to hear questions: both those that Jesus raises and answers. Who is Jesus Christ? What claims does he make of us? What is truly good or truly harmful for us? Is our love for others real, or mere talk?

Matthew, especially, wants his readers to experience the challenge of Jesus and the questions that he raises. He has added six direct questions to those in the Passion story which he found in Mark while dropping one of Mark's. The result, as Donald Selby notes, is two series of ten questions which add movement and drama to the two main parts of the story.[1] Taken together they form a dramatic outline of the Passion through which the reader can be in touch with the challenging claims of the crucified and risen Jesus, the Question God has raised for all humankind.

In the first series, which includes the anointing at Bethany, the Last Supper, the prayer at Gethsemane, and the arrest are:

1. The indignant disciples at the anointing: "Why this waste?"

2. Jesus' reply: "Why do you trouble the woman?"

3. Judas to the chief priests: "What will you give me if I deliver him to you?"

4. The disciples to Jesus: "Where will you have us prepare for you to eat the Passover?"

---

[1] Donald J. Selby *"Introduction to the New Testament"* (New York, 1971, Macmillan *or* London, 1971, Collier-Macmillan) 145-147.

5. The disciples on Jesus' announcement of his betrayal: "Is it I, Lord?"

6. And Judas, "Is it I, Master?"

7. Jesus to Peter in Gethsemane: "So you could not watch with me one hour?"

8. Later to the disciples: "Are you still sleeping and taking your rest?"

9. To Judas at the arrest: "Friend, why are you here?"

10. "Do you think that I cannot appeal to my Father, and he will send me more than twelve legions of angels? But how then should the scriptures be fulfilled, that it must be so?...Have you come out as against a robber, with swords and clubs to capture me?"

In the second series, which includes the trials before Caiaphas and Pilate, and the Crucifixion are:

1. The high priest to Jesus: "Have you no answer to make? What is it that these men testify against you?"

2. The high priest to the council: "Why do we still need witnesses? You have now heard this blasphemy. What is your judgment?"

3. To Jesus at the mocking: "Who is it that struck you?"

4. The chief priests to Judas at his repentance: "What is that to us?"

5. Pilate to Jesus: "Are you the King of the Jews?"

6. Again: "Do you not hear how many things they testify against you?"

7. Pilate to the people: "Whom do you want me to release for you, Barabbas or Jesus who is called Christ?"

8. Again, "Which of the two do you want me to release for you?"

9. Again: "Then what shall I do with Jesus who is called Christ?"

10. Again, in response to their cry for crucifixion: "Why, what evil has he done?"

7. THE TEMPTATION AND THE CROSS

Dying for the forgiveness of sins, Jesus overcomes the temptations that universally afflict humankind. Matthew's temptation narrative (4:1-11 = Lk 4:1-13) adumbrates the meaning of Jesus' death and resurrection. The cross is the victory of the Son of God. Three times, in the temptation narrative Satan calls into question the Sonship of Jesus. The temptations recall those which the Israelites experienced in their desert wanderings. Jesus is portrayed as recapitulating in his person the history of Israel, who had also been designated by God as his son (Ex 4:22-23). But whereas Israel son of God broke faith with God, Jesus Son of God renders to him perfect obedience.

Matthew's christological context for the temptation narrative is the following: Jesus, in the line of David (1:21), is the Son of God (2:15; 3:17); he has his origin in God (1:20) and is the one chosen to shepherd the eschatological people of God (2:6), for, empowered by God for the messianic ministry (3:16-17), he proves himself in confrontation with Satan to be perfectly obedient to the will of God (4:3-4, 5-7, 8-10); as the true Son of God, he saves his (God's) people from their sins (1:21). Matthew's temptation narrative portrays Jesus as the ideal Israelite, the Son of God, who bids his disciples to pray to God, "...thy will be done" (6:10), and announces to them that his true relatives are all who do the "will of my Father who is in heaven" (12:50), and warns them that only those will enter the kingdom of heaven who do the "will of my Father who is in heaven" (7:21; also 18:14).

Through the summons of Jesus Messiah, the Son of God, the disciples of Jesus become sons of God and brothers, and enter into the sphere of kingly rule. In response to his summons, the disciples reflects in their lives the will of God as Jesus makes it known in his ongoing confrontation with Satan and complete commitment to God, culminating in his death and resurrection.

Matthew makes it clear that encounter with Jesus places a person in a crisis decision (4:17; 10:34-35; 11:3-6, 14-15, 20; 13:9, 43; 21:31-32). In confrontation with the words and deeds of Jesus, a person faces the choice of "repenting" and "entering" the gracious sphere of the kingdom (see 4:17; 11:20; 21:31-32) or of rejecting Jesus as Messiah (see chapters 11—12). Matthew begins his Gospel by portraying Jesus as the Son of God in whom God has drawn near with his eschatological rule to dwell with his people (1:23). Matthew also portrays the arch-adversary of Jesus who stands in unmitigated opposition to the kingdom of heaven (cf. e.g. 6:10, 13; 11:12; 12:24-29; 13:39). Matthew attributes to Satan a "kingdom" (12:26), which means that he, too, governs human lives. The clash between Jesus Son of God and Satan, in Matthew's Gospel, is an ongoing one between the kingdom of heaven and the kingdom of Satan (the "Tempter" 4:3; "Beelzebul" 12:24, 27; the "Evil One" 13:19; the power through temptation: he tries to get them to live "lawlessly" (cf. 7:23; 13:41; 23:28; 24:12), that is, a manner which is contrary to the will of God (cf. 4:1-11; 6:13; 16:23; 27:40).

The kingdom of heaven and the kingdom of Satan possess in Matthew's Gospel the quality of "already... but not yet". Satan has already been overcome by the power of the kingdom at work in Jesus, but his capacity for evil has not yet been taken from him. The kingdom of heaven has already entered the world in Jesus the Son, but it has not yet been fully established in splendor to the total elimination of evil in human lives. Matthew's portraits of Jesus and Satan raise the questions for his readers: Where do we stand in the conflict between the two kingdoms? Is our security ultimately in God or elsewhere? Do we let God be God, accepting to live and die on his terms as Jesus has made them known, or have we opted to become a law unto ourselves?

Jesus' dying for the forgiveness of sins implies that our authentic commitment to God will cost us something. Just as God's forgiveness of our sins cost him the life of his Beloved Son, our fidelity to God in forgiving others will inevitably involve a kind of dying to ourselves. The temptation narrative implies Jesus' refusal to manipulate God for merely human ends. The disciple, like his Master, will reject the temptation to manipulate God for purposes of human pride. Jesus rejects Satan's proposal that he attract a following by assuming a spectacular appearance of danger while remaining perfectly safe in the divine power. He rejects the temptation to play-acting, to posturing as a spectacular savior, without having to pay the price in suffering and death. In his prayer at Gethsemane, Jesus asks that he might not have to drink the bitter cup of suffering, but adds "not my will, but thine be done" (26:39 = Lk 22:42). The temptation to messiahship without suffering, no less than the temptation to discipleship without suffering, must be rejected. Satan suggests that Jesus accomplish his mission by a painless "lifting up" and still thereby draw all to himself (see also John 3:13; 12:32), whereas the ultimate lifting up of Jesus will be agonizing, and not by ministering angels but by Roman mercenaries. As Jesus rejected much pretence from the beginning of his ministry to his crucifixion at the end, so he exhorted against it throughout his teaching. He condemns sham, such as doing good deeds to be seen by others (6:1); he warns that those who exalt themselves shall be humbled (18:4; 23:12). Jesus, consistently demanding that our commitment to God and neighbor be real, condemned the self-deception that salvation might be attained through mere appearances or posturing. He repeatedly emphasized the cost of discipleship. As in his teachings, so in his actions: rejecting Satan's enticement to a counterfeit display of sonship, he accepts the way of the cross to be revealed as the forgiving Son of God that he really is.

III. Luke

Essential to understanding the death of Jesus in Luke's Gospel is the recognition that the complex, life-death-resurrection-ascension/glorification, constitutes a whole whose individual parts find their full meaning in relation to the whole.

1. AN EXODUS AND AN ASCENSION

Luke alone describes the death of Jesus as an "exodus" (9:31) which culminates in an ascension into heaven (9:51). Luke alone employs the words *ëxodus* and *analēmpsis* (ascension) to explain the meaning of the Jesus-event. Moses and Elijah appear in glory at the Transfiguration of Jesus and speak of the exodus that he is to fulfill in Jerusalem (9:51). The Greek word *exodus* can be translated as *departure* and *destiny*. Peter, James, and John, who witness the event, become aware that the whole direction of the mission of Jesus from Galilee to Jerusalem is not a casual journey, but nothing less than a new exodus. Peter wants to mark the occasion by holding a feast of Tabernacles in which the Jews lived in tent-like shelters for seven days as a way of reenacting the exodus from Egypt and wanderings in the desert (See Lev 23:42-44); but it is wrong for him to want to keep Moses and Elijah in this way. He would be making Jesus just one more episode in the history of Israel; but Jesus *is* Israel personified, and it is time for Moses and Elijah to give way. What they have helped to create has appeared in the person of Jesus. Jesus is the new and greater Moses and the new and greater Elijah, bringing to fulfillment the Old Testament exodus and law and prophecy.

Luke, like other writers in the New Testament (John, and the authors of Hebrews and 1 Peter), has been powerfully influenced by the journey-theme in the Old Testament. He has constructed his two books with this picture in mind. The mission of Jesus is in the form of a journey up to Jerusalem, but Luke (like John) envisions this as a part of Jesus' journey up to the Father in the ascension. The climax of his Gospel is, deliberately, not the resurrection, but the ascension (24:51). In his second volume, Acts, Christ journeys in a new way. Through his Spirit he travels with Christians from Jerusalem to Rome, directing them on their journey, enabling them to share in his exodus and destiny.

A major division of Luke's Gospel begins with the announcement of Jesus' journey to Jerusalem. The narrative of the journey from Galilee to Jerusalem extends 9:51 to 19:57. Comparison of this section with the structure of the book of Deuteronomy suggests that Luke is recalling the exodus of Moses and the people of Israel to the borders of the promised land. In the temptation Jesus had a vision of himself brought to the top of Mount Pisgah to be shown the promised land (4:5-7). And the question as he saw it then remains the same. Shall he go in and possess it by quick decisive means (e.g. by force), or leave it to the Father to bring him in as and when he wills? There will be constant inducements to demand signs for discovering for certain "whether the Lord is among us or not" (see Ex 17:7). Those nearest to Jesus, like James and John, will, with the best intentions, urge him to try to make things certain for himself.

Luke interprets the death of Jesus as both an exodus or liberation from the power of darkness and an ascension into his glory. his journey is to the Holy City, the place where the Messiah would reign, the "throne of David." His move to kingship, whatever form that might take, must now begin in response to his Father's will. Luke deliberately puts, as a heading to the journey narrative, a reminder that there is more to this journey of Jesus than going to Jerusalem. It is already part of his ascension, when he was to be taken up to heaven: "As the time approached when he was to be taken up to heaven (*analēmpsis*), he set his face resolutely towards Jerusalem" (9:51).

Luke presents the entire life of Jesus as a life lived in complete conformity to the will of God. From the beginning, the boy Jesus declares that he must be occupied in the affairs of his Father (2:49). The mature Jesus states that he must preach the kingdom (4:43); he must be on his way (13:33). He declares again that the Son of Man must first suffer many things (17:25); that what has been written must be fulfilled in him (22:37). His life is a total process of exodus and ascension in conformity to the will of God; it is a process of overcoming evil and of entering into glory. His death, for Luke, is similarly both an exodus and an ascension; it is a moment in the process that the Father wills for the coming of his kingdom.

2. THE INNOCENT MARTYR

The death of Jesus, in Luke's account, is that of the innocent martyr. Pilate proclaims Jesus innocent three times (23:4, 14, 22), as do Herod (23:15), one of the criminals at the cross (23:41), and the centurion (23:47).

Perhaps his regard for Roman authorities and his apologetic motives may account for the way that Luke has transferred the mocking of Jesus from Pilate's soldiers to those of Herod (cf. 23:11 with Mk 15:16-20). The trial before Herod, unique to Luke, ends with an acknowledgement of Jesus' innocence (23:15), and Jesus is remanded to Pilate. In three solemn pronouncements, significantly more emphatic than Mark (cf. 23:14-15 with Mk 15:5), Pilate declares the innocence of Jesus. Pilate's hesitation is evidence of Jesus' innocence.

Jesus, the sinless and innocent martyr, is engaged in an apocalyptic struggle with evil. His death is an exodus, a deliverance, an eschatological triumph over the power of evil. After the third temptation (4:13) Satan leaves Jesus "until an opportune time" but returns during the Passion, entering into Judas (22:3). Satan is ready to capture Peter (22:31), and the Passion is the assault of the power of darkness. However, Satan's attacks are futile, both against the disciples and against Jesus. Unlike the Markan portrayal, the disciples do not fail during the Passion, but are described as "those who have continued with me in my trials" (22:28). The power of the innocent Jesus is implied in the efficacy of his prayer for Simon that his faith will not fail, even after the denial (22:32). Jesus is the model for those who suffer innocently; just as suffering did not destroy Jesus, neither will it destroy those who follow him (cf. 21:13-14).

The silence of Jesus, in Luke's Gospel, reflects the power

of the innocent one whose innocence speaks for itself (see Is 53:7, 9). Jesus refuses to speak in his own defense before Herod (23:9). Jesus' own temptations have shown that it is the spirit of Satan which prompts the demand for self-satisfying certainty. The spirit of God involves turning to God and keeping alert for *his* signs. But as the transfiguration incident has shown, Jesus is not one of the old prophets; he is the new Elijah and his mission is not to call for more signs, but to be the once-for-all sign himself.

Jesus implies his innocence when he speaks to the chief priests and captains of the Temple guard and elders who had come for him. He asks, "'Am I a brigand...that you had to set out with swords and clubs?'" (22:52). He protests that when he was among them daily in the Temple they had never threatened him. He then explains that "'this is your hour...the reign of darkness'" (22:53). (In John's Gospel, Jesus speaks of "my hour" of glorification; whereas, in Luke's Gospel, the Passion becomes "your hour," the hour of his enemies.) His death is an exodus or a deliverance from the power of his enemies. His goodness is that of the Just One who overpowers death itself. (His triumph over evil is a traditional theme found in Gal 1:4; Col 2:20; Hb 2:4). His death delivers a people from bondage and leads them to a new freedom before God, an ascension. "The power of darkness" began for Luke at Jesus' arrest and lasts until his death, his exodus.

The three hours of darkness preceding Jesus' death are an eschatological sign of judgment, announcing as a Passover symbol a divine judgment of salvation and condemnation. It is not to be identified with the "power of darkness" that represents Jesus' enemies and their power over him during his passion. Parodoxically, these three hours of darkness represent the end of their power. Just as in Egypt before the exodus the three days of darkness did not adversely affect the children of Israel but only the Egyptians (Ex 10:23), so at Golgotha the three hours of darkness do not adversely affect Jesus but only his enemies. This judgment of condemnation is symbolized by the tearing of the Temple veil; this judgment of salvation is symbolized in the confession of the centurion. The centurion's confession of faith in the "Just One" (23:47) represents the participation of the new people that Jesus has founded in and through his ascension.

3. THE TORN VEIL

Although Luke announces the rending of the Temple veil in almost the same words as Mark (Lk 23:45), he reports this event after his mention of the darkness. The rending of the veil occurs *before* Jesus' death. In Mark the torn veil is a direct and immediate result of Jesus' death. The rending of the veil, in all the Synoptic accounts, follows the darkness and symbolizes the judgment of condemnation which represents the end of the old covenant and its liturgy. Since there is not mention in Luke of the destruction of the temple at the religious trial or in the mocking scene, the torn veil is even more symbolic of the saving judgment which inaugurates the new covenant and a direct access to God in Jesus Christ for all humankind.

The rending of the veil between the moment when Jesus promises the Good Thief that they will be together in paradise and the moment when Jesus dies suggests that what God is accomplishing at Golgotha is the creation of a passageway for Jesus to enter into the heavenly sanctuary. This squares with Luke's exodus and ascension theology. Jesus' death in Mark and Matthew is a "going away" (Mk 14:21; Mt 26:24); only in Luke is it an exodus from the power of darkness and an ascension into glory, a being taken up from this life and this world into a new life and a new world. When Luke, therefore, reports the rending of the veil after Jesus' promise to the Good Thief, he is presenting it as a symbol of new passageway into the Holy of Holies (= God's presence = paradise), that God has created through the death of Jesus for the entrance of the Good Thief and of all whom he represents.

The opening of the veil before the death of Jesus symbolizes Jesus' recognition of the moment of his exodus and ascension, when he cries out and entrusts his spirit to his Father. Jesus is the first to pass through the veil with the

Good Thief, the representative of all who are to follow by acknowledging Jesus as king. Being with Jesus is to be with God in paradise, where the just go after death. Only through the death of Jesus can we have life with Jesus; only through sharing his death can we share his life with God; only through sharing his exodus can we share his ascension.

4. TWO WORDS OF MERCY

In Mark and Matthew, Jesus speaks only once from the cross. In Luke Jesus speaks three times and, typically for Luke, they are words of mercy and of trust in the Father. Luke repeats the same idea on the lips of Stephen (Acts 7:59-60), where the true disciple witnesses his master in martyrdom. In Greek, the past tense or imperfect is used, suggesting that when Jesus said, "'Father, forgive them,'" (*elegen* in 23:34), he was saying it repeatedly. The dying Jesus is the living image or matrix for the Good Thief's insight into his identity, recalling Mark's centurion, who "*seeing how he died*, confessed." (Mk 15:39). Luke's "'Father, forgive'" makes more precise what Christians see in their crucified Lord: Jesus dies as the *son* of a merciful Father from whom he asks mercy for others. He dies showing the meaning of his words, "'Love your enemies, do good to those who hate you, bless those who curse you, pray for those who abuse you... Be merciful, even as your Father is merciful'" (6:27, 36).

Luke implies the efficacy of Jesus' prayer "'Father, forgive them,'" in its impact on the Good Thief, on the centurion who saw what had taken place, and on the people who had gathered for the spectacle... The Good Thief recognizes the innocence of Jesus in contrast with his own guilt, the messianic hope that Jesus offers in contrast with his own hopelessness, and prays that Jesus save him. His words, "'remember me when you come into your kingdom'" (23:42), have a messianic meaning that is underscored in the promise of paradise which Jesus makes to him, in his second word from the cross: "'I promise you... today you will be with me in paradise'" (23:43). The merciful Messiah admits the Good Thief into his messianic kingdom. (Luke contrasts the purely temporal interpretations of the messianic kingdom, which characterizes those who tell Jesus to save himself from the cross, with the true interpretation of the man who, despite the apparent hopelessness of his situation, hopes that Jesus will remember [= save] him).

Only Luke tells us that the centurion "praised God" before he made his confession that "'Truly this man was the Just One'" (23:47). His confession of faith, made without the help of apocalyptic signs, glorifies God. Only Luke shows the many witnesses to the execution returning home beating their breasts (23:48). The kingdom comes, for Luke, with a change of heart in the people that is the result of the merciful action of the Father in the exodus and ascension of his son. The only signs that Luke has follow upon the death of Jesus are interior signs of faith, repentance, and conversion, unlike Mark and Matthew, who have exterior signs. This squares with Luke's emphasis on conversion and repentance throughout his Passion narrative (Peter, the women of Jerusalem, the Good Thief, the centurion, the witnesses beating their breasts). For Luke, the kingdom comes with the change of heart in the people, an event no less real than an earthquake. Their repentance is the effect of Jesus' death (see Acts 2).

"Father, forgive them" is Luke's key-to-character statement of Jesus as the Good News of a merciful Father for all humankind. A true child of God is recognized, as Jesus is recognized, by the quality of mercy and compassion for others. Because the heavenly Father is merciful and compassionate, his true children will, as a matter of course, be recognized by their likeness to him. Luke alone of the Synoptics, a moment before the climax of his Gospel of mercy, shows Jesus repeating the two words that sum up his message and meaning and mission: "Father, forgive." This answers the question that followed Jesus throughout his life: "Who are you?" He is the merciful Son of the merciful Father, whose kingdom comes with repentance, total conversion of mind and heart, a freedom *from* self-centeredness and a freedom *for* a merciful God and our neighbor, manifested in deeds of mercy and compassion. Luke brings out the deeper meaning of the apocalyptic details that mark the coming of the kingdom in the other Synoptic accounts of Jesus' death. His willingness to die of such compassionate and merciful love for all reveals the total commitment of the Son to his merciful Father: "'Father, into your hands I commit my spirit'" (23:46).

The Good Thief symbolizes all who confess the kingship of Jesus and are being taken with him in the exodus-ascension process into the presence of his Father (paradise). He symbolizes those who are being delivered from their bondage to sin through their commitment to Jesus Christ, the Just One (23:47).

5. THE FINAL WORD: PSALM 31

"'Father, into your hands I commit my spirit'" (23:46), the final words of Jesus are taken from Psalm 31 (30):5. Luke has added the word, "Father," which most characterized all the prayers of Jesus. The prayer occurs after the darkness ends at the ninth hour (23:44). This is the time of the evening sacrifice in the Temple accompanied by the evening prayer. The preparation for this sacrifice had been under way from about 2:30 p.m. to 3:00 p.m.; the trumpets of the Temple sounded to call the people to prayer. This temporal context gives a special significance to Luke's use of Psalm 31(30):5; for this Psalm was used privately as the pious Jew's evening or night prayer. Before going to sleep, pious Jews prayed, "Into your hands I commit my spirit." Luke's reference to the ninth hour, followed by the rending of the Temple veil, contextualizes Jesus' prayer with the implication that it is the ultimate expression of the prayer of Israel. Luke portrays Jesus as praying with his people. The customary prayer before a night's sleep is said before Jesus' sleep of death. Inasmuch as the Passover ends when the last participant goes to sleep, Luke suggests that the death (sleep) of Jesus brings to completion the meaning of the historical Jewish Passover, no less than the historical Last Supper of Jesus with his disciples. In the language of John's

Gospel, "'It is consummated'" (19:30).

The rending of the Temple veil *before* Jesus' death suggests that Jesus dies in the presence of his Father. No sooner are we told that the veil is torn than Jesus cries out in a loud voice, entrusting himself to the Father into whose presence he has just entered in the glory of his ascension. He had just promised the penitent thief that "today" they would be together in paradise. Luke alone describes the death of Jesus in words which express his passing over from this life to the next, as an exodus completed in his death and more than an arrival at the brink of the promised land. Unlike Moses, Jesus enters into the promised land; he is assumed by his Father into glory. His final words encompass both his exodus and ascension into the fullness of his Father's glory. He has completed his exodus from the power of darkness and entered into paradise and into his Father's hands. The risen Christ expresses this exodus and ascension to the disciples on their way to Emmaus: "'Was it not necessary for the Christ to suffer these things and enter into his glory?'" (24:26). His bodily resurrection occurs three days after his death and his bodily ascension occurs forty days later (see Lk 24: 1-6; Acts 1: 1-9).

Jesus dies with words of filial trust. Luke sees in the death of Jesus the way every Christian should live and die. He emphasizes Jesus' complete commitment to his Father in freedom and love. Stephen, at his death, commits himself to Jesus in similar words: "'Lord Jesus, receive my spirit'" (Acts 7:59).

Jesus' entire life mediated the merciful compassion of God, so it is not surprising that Luke should place words of forgiveness on his lips during his final hours. Jesus dies as the just and merciful Savior who continues to welcome sinners (the Good Thief) to the very end and then commends his soul to his merciful Father. Jesus' promise of paradise to the Good Thief implies that when Jesus commends his soul to his Father he is also commending the souls of all who, like the penitent thief and the martyred Stephen, have committed their lives to him. ("Soul" is used here in a biblical and not a Greek philosophical sense.)

By making Psalm 31(30):5 the last word of Jesus, Luke emphasizes that Jesus dies in the presence of the Father whom he has made immediately and directly accessible to all. Through the exodus and ascension of Jesus we have direct access to the Father.

6. THE TEMPTATION AND THE CROSS

Jesus dies with a filial trust that both fulfills his mission and reveals his method for overcoming "the reign of darkness" (22:52). The exodus and the ascension of Jesus entail both a struggle against and a victory over the powers of darkness. The temptation narrative reveals the strategy of the devil or the powers of darkness. (The temptation is reported in only summary form in Mark 1:12-13 and in a fuller form in Matthew 4:1-11 and Luke 4:1-13). The temptation episode describes the kind of Messiah Jesus is, and by implication what kind of society the Church, the new Israel is called to be: it lives by the word of God, it does not challenge God's promises, and it adores and serves God alone and not the world. Jesus rejects in anticipation the temptations to which his Church will be submitted.

The devil seeks to undermine Jesus' radical trust in his Father. The temptation episode occurs as a sequel to Jesus' baptism. Jesus knows his unique vocation and rejects all unworthy interpretations of his baptismal experience in which he had heard the heavenly voice affirming, "'You are my Son, my Beloved.'" — Now Jesus hears another voice, "'If you are the Son of God...'" and he must discern whether that voice comes from the same source. That voice proffers advice for his messianic mission. Three times Jesus concludes that the voice which prompts him to action is that of the devil. The methods for the coming of the kingdom are not those of the voice that he had heard at his baptism. That voice alone merits his filial trust.

All the replies that Jesus gives to the devil in the temptation episode come from that section of the book of Deuteronomy (chs. 6-8) which is concerned with God's summons to Israel and Israel's temptation to disregard it by trusting in itself rather than in God, who alone is absolutely trustworthy. Following Luke's order of temptations, Jesus was tempted to anticipate, for his own satisfaction, the bounty which the Father would give, but in his own time and way: "'If you are the Son of God, tell this stone to become bread'" (4:3). But the first of the many trials of Jesus as he sets out to realize the destiny of Israel is overcome; he does not put his Father to the test because of his absolute trust in him. The second temptation concerns how Jesus is to receive a kingdom. Was it something exclusively his to take as and when he would (as the devil suggests), or was it something which his Father would bestow on him? The new Israel in Jesus overcomes idolatry (see Dt. 8:17-19). Finally, Jesus is faced with Israel's basic and continuing temptation, to demand a sign from heaven which would make it unequivocally clear whether the Lord is among us or not (Ex 17:7). Jesus entrusts himself to his Father. He does not doubt his Father. There is no need to put his Father to test. His Father will proclaim him in his own time and way: in his exodus and ascension on Golgotha.

IV. John

John's passion narrative is the shortest of the accounts and, although it has points of contact with the Synoptics, is not directly dependent on them. The theological interpretation of Jesus' death emerges not only from the narrative itself, but also from the farewell discourses (chs. 14-17), which function as an extended commentary on the Passion. John softens the harsher aspects of Jesus' suffering by reducing the scourging and mocking to two verses (19: 2-3). The suffering and death of Jesus is less a story of degradation than the triumphal return of the Word to the Father and the hour of glorification (17:1), as well as the prelude to the sending of the Spirit (= Advocate = Paraclete = Helper), who will teach the disciples all truth and bring to their minds what Jesus has told them (14:26; 16:13).

1. AUTHORITY AND MAJESTY

Authority and majesty characterize Jesus in John's passion narrative. The suffering and death of Jesus is a victory, though the world does not understand it as such. At his arrest Jesus knows what is to befall him (18:4), and his captors fall before his majesty (18:6). He has the power to protect his disciples (18:8-9; cf. 17:12). We read nothing of the agony in the garden. His death is the willing acceptance of the cup his Father has given him (18:11). In the hearing before the Jewish officials, in contrast to the silence or cryptic answers in the Synoptics, Jesus interrogates his captors (18:20-24). We read only a minimum of the indignities shown Jesus by his judges. In the Pilate sequence Jesus confounds the powers of the world (19: 10-11) and Pilate is reduced to the role of powerless questioner (18:38; 19:9). From beginning to end, and not only in the resurrection and giving of the Spirit, John sees the Passion as the story of Christ's glorification (18:1-20:31). Even when Jesus is crowned with thorns, it is as a king. John presents the death of the revealer, the royal witness to the truth, who continues to the end to complete his saving work in obedience to his Father's will. Jesus overcomes the powers of the world (cf. 15:18-26), as a model of love, the good shepherd who lays down his life (cf. 10:1-18), and in his being lifted up, draws all humankind to himself (cf. 12:32; 8:28).

His crucifixion is his exaltation (3:14; 8:28; 12:32), an eschatological victory over the cosmos and its ruler. Jesus is bringing his work to completion, even in the final instructions he gives from the cross. He is willing to be lifted up so that all who believe in him may have eternal life (3:14-15). He gives his flesh for the life of the world (6:51). Like the seed that both dies and bears fruit (12:24), the death of Jesus is a life-giving and triumphal return to the Father (13:1; 16:28), an exaltation for the benefit of all humankind. Through his death we have been given the gift of eternal life, a personal knowledge that begets love of the only true God, and the Son whom he has sent (17:3), so that we know the "kingship" of God and his Son in the love which "rules" (motivates, directs, inspires) our hearts and "governs" our lives. The ultimate authority and majesty of God is gloriously revealed in the love of the Son lifted up and laying down his life for his friends (cf. 15:13). John's account of Jesus' suffering and death is implicitly a description of the meaning of divine and human love, of how the true God and his Son have loved us "to the end" (13:1) as the authors of their love in our lives.

2. CONTINUITY AND CLIMAX

John introduces his account of the passion and death of Jesus with an explicit statement that the narrative of the death of Jesus that follows is a continuation of the life that had gone before: "Now before the feast of the Passover, when Jesus knew that his hour had come to depart from this world to the Father, having loved his own who were in the world, he loved them unto the end" (13:1). John portrays the final events of Jesus' passion and death as a continuation "unto the end" of a love that they had already known. John symbolizes this love in Jesus' washing of his disciples' feet. Jesus explains to his disciples that this action expresses how he understands his relationship to them, and how they should understand their relationship to one another (13:15). Though he is their "teacher and lord," he is among them as one who serves. This episode interprets the life of Jesus that has gone before, and the death that awaits him the next day. It interprets the love that he is showing them "unto the end" as a love of service. Although Jesus had washed Judas' feet, he can say that Judas was not clean (13:10). The external cleansing is symbolic of an internal cleansing, which Judas would not accept and which could have no effect without his consent. Jesus' action symbolizes his utter commitment in freedom and love to the work which his Father has sent him to do (4:34; 17:4). To share Jesus' total commitment to the service of the Father in freedom and love is to be internally transformed or "cleansed." Jesus' action of washing his disciples' feet symbolizes his living and dying for his Father (cf. 4:34; 14:31; 17:4) and his friends (15:13). The Father wills that Jesus befriend them. Jesus serves his Father by befriending them. To be cleansed or transformed is the lived knowledge that the Father has befriended us in the befriending life and death of Jesus: "'I call you friends, because I have made known to you everything that I have learnt from my Father'" (15:15).

John interprets the death of Jesus not only as the continuation of Jesus' life, but also as its climax and culmination. There is no greater love than laying down one's life for one's friends (15:13). By interpreting Jesus' death as the culmination of his life, John is saying that Jesus is most characteristically Jesus in the giving of his befriending life to the very limits of which love is capable. For John, Jesus is not passive in dying, and his death is not something just inflicted on him. Rather, in his death, Jesus is most active, most personal, most free. The cross for John represents, not an act of dying, but an act of living: a life-giving event, an affirmation of eternal life (17:3) and the ultimate triumph of interpersonal divine and human love even in the face of death.

Jesus' washing of his disciples' feet is reminiscent of God himself, as described by Ezechiel, who takes pity on his beloved Jerusalem and cleanses her with water when no one else would do it (Ez 16:1-9). What Jesus is doing symbolizes God's love for his beloved people, the time of his loving action on their behalf: "Your time had come, the time for love. I spread part of my cloak over you and covered your nakedness; I bound myself by oath, I made a covenant with you — it is the Lord Yahweh who speaks — and you became mine. I bathed you in water, I washed the blood off you, I anointed you with oil" (Ez 16:8-9). The God of Israel is doing in Jesus Christ, what the prophet of Israel, Ezekiel, knew he would do when "the time for love" had arrived.

Looking back at the earlier parts of John's Gospel, we recognize that this theme is at work in his story of the good shepherd who lays down his life for his sheep in order "'that they may have life, and have it abundantly'" (10:11). John's image of Jesus as the good shepherd is a clear allusion to and interpretation of the death of Jesus as his self-giving for others, a sign that the God of Israel's "time for love" had arrived.

John's story of the raising of Lazarus (11:1-44) is another sign that this time has arrived; for it includes a strong emphasis on the love and compassion of Jesus. He first receives news of the illness of Lazarus with the message: "'Lord, he whom you love is ill.'" When he arrives at the scene and sees Mary and the others weeping "he was deeply moved in spirit and troubled," and "wept," so that the Jews said: "See how he loved him." Finally, John says that when Jesus came to the tomb he was "deeply moved again." In the variety of motifs that run through the story, sign and glorification, resurrection and life, belief and disbelief, John's narrative puts great emphasis on the love and compassion which Jesus had for Lazarus and his two sisters. This is not the same image of Jesus as when the synoptics spoke of the compassion of Jesus, for it is a more personal love than when Jesus had "compassion for the multitude." In John's image of Jesus' love and compassion for Lazarus and his sisters we see God's love for humankind in a human image. Jesus' entire life, and especially his death, images God's love: the reciprocal love of Father and Son, and their love for all humankind.

The key theological word that describes the death of Jesus in John is "accomplished" (= "completed," "fulfilled," "finished"). This word (Greek: *teleioun*) occurs three times in the passage 19:28-30. Jesus dies with the knowledge that he has completed his mission; he has fulfilled his Father's will in communicating their "eternal life" (cf. 17:3). Jesus has the knowledge of the revealer who knows his task and how it is accomplished. His final words, "'It is accomplished,'" are the signature to his entire life-work and to his revelation of God which attains its climax in this death that is the perfection of divine and human love: "He bowed his head, and gave up his spirit" (19:30). (Literally, Jesus "handed over" his spirit). He has lived and died that we might have his spirit.

3. SENDING THE HELPER

In John's Gospel, Jesus promises his disciples that in answer to his prayer the Father will give them "another Paraclete" (14:16). This implies that Jesus himself is primarily the Paraclete, or Helper, for the Spirit who is sent is "another" Paraclete. The Holy Spirit is the Helper whose function is identified with the mission of Jesus, but who is yet distinguished from him. John's use of masculine pronouns and adjectives (14:16: "another"; 14:26: "he"; 16:13: "he") shows that the Spirit is regarded as fully personal. These passages present the personality of the Spirit of God as that of the Helper. He is the Spirit of truth (14:16), who is the guide to Jesus. He will teach the disciples all truth and bring to their minds what Jesus has told them (14:26; 16:13). He will bear witness to Jesus (15:26). He will demonstrate the error of the world concerning sin, righteousness, and judgment (16:6-11). He will give glory to Jesus (16:14).

John's Gospel has a kind of trinitarian structure. It begins with Two who are eternal in God, one of whom becomes Man, and it continues through the first part of the Gospel on the relations of the Two, now known as Father and Son. But, with his death now imminent, the Son introduces the Holy Spirit, the Helper, whom he will send in his stead. The farewell discourse gives an explanation of the promised Holy Spirit's mission. Finally, the crucified and glorified Christ breathes his indwelling Spirit upon his disciples in a new act of creation (20:22). The coming of the indwelling Spirit to Jesus' followers is both dependent and consequent upon the completion of the saving work of Jesus himself in his death and resurrection, which together signify his exaltation (cf. 7:39). Hence the coming and the work of the Spirit are spoken of in the future tense throughout, and the promise of the gift of "another Paraclete" is fulfilled only when Jesus has been glorified (cf. 7:39; 15:26).

Jesus' death, resurrection, exaltation and sending of the Spirit are closely associated in John's Gospel. "Exaltation" (the "lifting up") is an expression with two meanings in the Fourth Gospel. It describes the exaltation on the cross as well as the exaltation to the Father (3:14; 8:28; 12:32), the glorification (7:39; 12:16). Jesus' death on the cross represents both his departure to his Father (13:1) and his entry into eternal glory (17:5). Therefore the Risen Christ appears to Mary Magdalen on the way to his Father, as ascending to his Father (20:17). Raised in exaltation to his Father in the event of the cross, he possesses all power and can draw everything to himself (12:32). For John the cross is glory because it reveals most fully what God is and does in the reciprocal love of Father and Son. On the cross, Jesus gives their Holy Spirit — the power of their reciprocal love that can draw everything and everyone — to all who believe in him. Jesus' giving up his life coincides with his giving us his Spirit. (This does not conflict with the reception of the Spirit by Jesus' disciples on the evening of his resurrection (20:21-23), when he gives his Spirit to a special group for a special purpose: the forgiveness of sins.) The Holy Spirit is that of both the Father and Son. Both bestow their life on us in their gift of their Holy Spirit (14:24, 26; 15:26).

4. THE NEW COMMUNITY OF FRIENDS

The bond which unites the body of believers to one another and to Christ and the Father is love: the Father's love for the Son and for those who belong to him, and their love responding to it (14:21; 15:10; 17:23, 26). Love, the motive behind the entire ministry of Jesus (3:16-17), is supremely shown and communicated by Jesus' giving his Spirit at the moment of his death (15:13 and 19:30). The gift of the Spirit enables the body of believers to continue the ministry of Jesus with the same love that grounded his interpersonal life with the Father (eternal life) and all humankind. The union of mutual love among the disciples is a sign of the loving union of the Father and Son (15:9-10) and, by implication, evidence that they have accepted the gift of their Holy Spirit. Their union of mutual love is God's gift of "glory" which Jesus has received from the Father and, in turn, has given to his disciples (17:21-23); it is evidence that they are sharing the interpersonal life of the Father and Son in their Spirit.

Jesus would make us friends, his friends and friends of the Father (15:13-15; 16:26-27). Friends, radically, because we have been initiated into the secrets of his heart, initiated by the Spirit, but friends authentically only if we respond to this revelation of love, respond by faith and love. The Spirit effects the union of the believer with the Son and thereby with the Father. He effects it with water and confirms it with his teaching (3:5; 16:13-14). The Spirit does not come alone, but brings the Father and the Son, who will together make their home with the believer (14:23), making their befriending presence and activity known to all humankind through the reciprocity of friendship within the community of believers (13:35). By accepting the gift of the Spirit the community of believers also manifests God's love for the world by continuing the universally befriending ministry of the only begotten Son, in order that all who believe in him may not perish but may have eternal life (3:16). The universally befriending love of the body of faith will recall that Jesus' love is all-embracing, that his flesh is given for the life of the world (6:51).

John represents what the befriending love of God is doing for humankind in his story of the raising of Lazarus (Jn 11). John pictures Lazarus and his two sisters as close friends of Jesus (11:3,5). When Jesus hears that Lazarus is ill, he says that it is not an "illness unto death" and delays two days before going to his friend. Only when it is certain that Lazarus is dead does Jesus go to Bethany with his disciples (11:14-15). Martha greets him with the words that Lazarus would not have died had Jesus been there sooner. When Jesus assures her that Lazarus will rise again, Martha shows her belief in the traditional Jewish view of a future resurrection, saying that she knows Lazarus will "'rise again in the resurrection of the last day'" (11:24). Jesus reinterprets her traditional view with his reply: "'I am the resurrection and the life; he who believes in me, though he die, yet shall he live, and whoever lives and believes in me shall never die'" (11:26). This statement summarizes the view of eternal life throughout the entire Gospel of John. Jesus gives eternal life *now* to those who believe in him; those who believe, though they suffer physical death, will never lose the eternal life (the reciprocal love of the Father and Son) that God bestows on them through Jesus and the gift of their Spirit. The Father befriends the friends of his Son.

The "I am" saying of Jesus, followed by Martha's confession of faith, provides a clue for the meaning of the sign. "I am" (Greek: *ego eimi*) is a technical phrase as a name for God in the Greek translation of Isaiah. John uses it to signify the presence of God himself in the person of Jesus. "'I am the resurrection and the life'" means that God himself is already with believers, sharing his eternal life with them. John has the High Priest unwittingly prophesy the gathering together of the children of God through the death and resurrection of Jesus, when he says that one man must die for the people that the whole nation should not perish (11:50). Not only the Jews who believe, but all the children of God scattered abroad, are to be gathered into one community (11:51-52) of life. God calls all through Jesus to the eternal life that no one can take from them, for he is its source (10:25-30).

The death of Jesus manifests and communicates the befriending love that creates and sustains the new community of eternal friendship: God's love for the world and Jesus' love for his own and all who are in the world; the Father's love for the Son and the Son's love for the Father. Jesus' giving of his Spirit (19:30) marks the accomplishment of his Father's will for the befriending of all humankind in the community of new life.

5. THE SEAMLESS GARMENT

All the Gospels mention the distribution of Jesus' garments. The soldiers were entitled to the executed person's possessions as a reward. Behind all the accounts looms the typically messianic Psalm 21(22):19, which John quotes explicitly (19:24): "They parted my garments among them, and for my clothing they cast lots." (Mark cites Psalm

21(22) as the "fourth word" of Jesus from the cross). Only John speaks of the "seamless garment" (19:23) worn by Jesus. The robe of the high priest is described in similar terms by Josephus, and rabbinic tradition also associates seamless robes with Moses and Adam. Possibly, John insinuates Jesus' priestly character, since it was forbidden to tear the high priest's garment (Lv 21:10). He may also have in mind the tunic of Joseph (Gn 37:3), a type of Christ as one betrayed by his brothers and yet their Savior (cf. Acts 7:9-11). The Fathers who saw in the seamless garment a symbol of the unity of the Church, the heritage of Jesus and his gift of the Spirit, contrasted with the division his coming had meant for the Jews (7:43; 9:16; 10:19), may have correctly perceived John's meaning.

6. THE SON'S LOVE

John alone tells us that Mary, Jesus' mother, stood by the cross (19:25). Only John has the words of Jesus commending his mother to the care of the beloved disciple (19:26-27). The Son's love, expressed in these words, brings a new family into being. If the unity of the Church, the new family, is symbolized by the seamless garment, the particular nature of that unity proceeds from the self-oblation of the Son of God and the communication of his Spirit in filial love with respect to his heavenly Father and human mother. The Son's love integrates humankind under the sovereignty of his Father's love. The reciprocal love of Father and Son is expressed throughout the farewell discourse; the implication of this love for all humankind is expressed in Jesus' concern for his mother. The love that proceeds from the Father is the Son's love for both his heavenly Father and for humankind. John brackets his passion narrative with the theme of the Son's love, recalling the theme of the Synoptics that those who hear the word of God and keep it are the true family of the Son of God (Mk 3:35; Mt 12:50; Lk 8:21).

When Jesus begins his mission at the wedding feast of Cana, he tells his mother to leave him alone because his hour has not come (2:4). When Jesus completes his mission on

Calvary, his hour has come for the revelation of the deepest meaning of his relationship with his mother. When the cross manifests completely the Father's love for humankind, the ultimate meaning and fulfillment of Mary's maternity is revealed in the birth of the new family of God. Jesus shares his heavenly Father and human mother with all humankind, after having promised that when he was lifted up on the cross he would draw everyone to himself (12:32). The Son's love for his heavenly Father and human mother unifies the family of God.

7. "I THIRST"

The piercing of Jesus' side (19:31-37), a narrative peculiar to John, is accompanied by an outpouring of blood and water. The event is linked with Jesus' words just before his death, "'I thirst'" (19:28). With these words, John recalls passages of the Psalms, the prayers of Israel, that express Israel's thirst for God: "My soul thirsts for God, the God of life; when whall I go to see the face of God?" i.e. to enjoy the presence of God in the Temple of Jerusalem (Ps 41[42]:2). Again: "God, you are my God, I am seeking you, my soul is thirsting for you, my flesh is longing for you, a land parched, weary and waterless; I long to gaze on you in the Sanctuary, and to see your power and glory. Your love is better than life itself" (Ps 62[63]:3). Water symbolizes the God for whom Jesus (Israel) thirsts, with whom Jesus is one, and whom he communicates to all through his life-giving death. The effusion of blood and water has a sacramental significance, which recalls the statement of 1 John 5:6-7:

> This is he who came by water and blood, Jesus Christ, not with the water only but with the water and the blood. And the Spirit is the witness, because the Spirit is the truth. there are three witnesses, the Spirit, the water, and the blood; and these three agree.

Jesus' witness came in his entire Spirit-directed mission, begun in water beside the Jordan and consummated in blood upon Golgotha, that of Christians, likewise Spirit-guided, must begin in the water of baptism and continue through the blood of the Eucharist so that our lives are lived as a continuing witness to that Love which alone can quench the thirst of all humankind.

Significantly, the "I thirst" of John's dying Jesus reminds us that all the Evangelists portray Jesus dying with a psalm on his lips. The Evangelists employ the traditional prayers of Israel to interpret the ultimate meaning of Jesus' life and death. They implicitly interpret Jesus' entire life and death as the prayer of Israel, of the people of God. In the light of the crucified and risen Christ and his gift of the Holy Spirit, they know that God has heard and answered Israel's prayer for the salvation of all humankind.

Knowing the importance of a dying man's words, the Evangelist selects them from the particular psalm which best expresses the deepest meaning of his entire narrative about Jesus' living and dying in God's love. Psalms 21(22) (Mark and Matthew), 30(31) (Luke), 41(42) and 62(63) (John) — all epitomize the Evangelist's theological interpretation of Jesus within the context of his gospel narrative. Each gospel narrative interprets the psalm and the psalm, in turn, epitomizes the meaning of the particular narrative. One illuminates the other.

Inasmuch as nothing is adequately understood outside of its context, we must therefore interpret the words or verse of the psalm uttered by the dying Jesus within the context of the entire psalm which, in turn, must be interpreted within the context of the particular gospel narrative. Both these contexts find their meaning within a third context — the prayer life or worship of the people of God — that is indispensable for a true understanding of the gospel narrative and its components.

The Jewish scriptures and their psalms (Old Testament) are the Bible and prayers of the first Christians in the decades that preceded the first New Testament writings. Interpreted in the light of the crucified and risen Christ and his Spirit, they are central to Christian worship. The evangelist reads these scriptures and prays these psalms both in his private and public worship. He writes as a worshiper for worshipers who share the same Jewish scriptures and psalms. He writes for worshipers who are accustomed to recite an entire psalm, when their leader recites the first verse, inviting them to join him.

Consequently, when Christian worshipers heard, for example, the words of Mark's Gospel taken from the first verse of Psalm 21(22), "'My God, my God, why have you deserted me?'" we may assume that their spontaneous response was to recognize the invitation of their crucified and risen Lord to pray the entire psalm with him, to share his life of fidelity and to hope in God, whatever the cost in suffering. When Mark prayed that psalm in the Christian assembly or in private, he inevitably recognized the voice of the psalmist as that of his crucified and risen Lord, before he ever employed its first verse as Jesus' dying word. He shares, at least implicitly, his prayer experience with the readers of his gospel narrative. This psalm that he prayed influenced, either directly or subliminally, the shape of his gospel narrative. Mark's Gospel invites Christians to accept, in freedom and love, Jesus' costly commitment to God in the service of all. Mark sees Jesus in the sufferings and hope of the Just One in Psalm 21(22); consequently, he concludes Jesus' life story with the words of the Just One. Mark wants his readers to hear the crucified and risen Jesus, the Just One of Israel, inviting them to share his way of the cross with the confidence that God will not hide his face from them (Ps 21[22]:24). With the words of the psalm, Mark implies that Jesus' entire life and death and new life are the continuous prayer of the Just One of the people of God. Jesus leads and calls — as the crucified and risen Just One — all humankind to the prayer that is his life commitment to God in the service of all. Similarly, each Evangelist employing psalms for the last words of his crucified and risen Lord, implicitly invites his readers to make the life-prayer of the Just One their own. The psalms the evangelists prayed either directly or subliminally influenced the shape of their gospel narrative.

8. TRINITARIAN LOVE

That love which endures forever, for John, is a way of being and doing and seeing with others that is revealed in the life and death and resurrection of Jesus Christ. His interpersonal life of equality with the Father and their Spirit reveals that God is a community of three persons in love. Their interpersonal love is the "eternal life" of which John writes that transcends mere immortality. There is a trinitarian import in John's account of the passion and death of Jesus which underlies his affirmation that God is love.

The Father and the Son, for John, are neither seen nor experienced apart from one another; for seeing the Son is seeing the Father. They are simultaneously known; and they are known in what they are simultaneously doing. The loving Father is seen in his giving his life to his Son; the beloved Son is seen in his receiving his life from his Father. The community of Christian faith knows the Father and the Son as two distinct persons in their reciprocity of one life and love, their Holy Spirit, given to the community.

John's account of Calvary implies that the Father and Son are seen in the giving and receiving of their Spirit (life and love) that unites John and Mary to one another in the dynamic of their Trinitarian love. The reciprocity of the Father and Son is manifested in the reciprocity of the mother and son. The dying Jesus imparts his Spirit to his mother and beloved disciple. By communicating to them the love and life that he and his Father share, Jesus enables their new way of being and doing and seeing with others. Through the transforming gift of the Spirit of the Father and Son — interpersonal, Trinitarian life and love — Mary sees John as her son and John sees Mary as his mother. They experience themselves in Trinitarian love as being given to one another. They are one in the life and love of the one interpersonal God, while remaining distinct persons within that life and love of three distinct Persons. They accept and identify themselves in that Trinitarian dynamic of interpersonal love transforming their being and doing and seeing.

Just as the Father is seen in the Son, the Father and Son are seen or experienced in the giving and receiving of their

Holy Spirit, of the life and love that unite them and the community of Christian faith. John and Mary at Calvary are the Fourth Gospel's icon of Trinitarian love. The Son, whose filial love unites him to his heavenly Father and human mother, reveals the Father and what they are doing when he gives his mother and beloved disciple to one another. The Son imparts his Spirit — the life and love he shares with his heavenly Father — to them to enable them to become what he and, implicitly, his Father have called them to be for one another in Trinitarian love. John and Mary represent the community of faith that lives in that Spirit and prays the "Our Father" knowing that they have been given to one another by the Father and Son through the gift of their Spirit. In the real love that we have for one another, we know the love of the Three persons; we live in the Spirit that is the love Father and Son have for one another.

If the Holy Trinity does in our lives what it does in its own, the Father in you is giving himself to the Son in me and the Father in me is giving himself to the Son in you. The Son in you is welcoming life from the Father in me and the Son in me is welcoming life from the Father in you. We are bonded as brothers and sisters by/in the Spirit of the life-giving Father and life-welcoming Son. We are given to one another in and through the Spirit of the love-giving Father and his love-welcoming Son, The Beloved. We know, or 'see,' in the reciprocity of love within the Christian community the Spirit of the Father's and Son's love that has been given to us. Intrapersonally, the Three persons are present and active and communicating in individuals, relating them interpersonally and socially in the Father-Son-Spirit dynamic. ("Brother" and/or "Sister" might describe the Spirit in this relationship; for we are bonded together as brothers and sisters through our participation in the giving and welcoming of the Father and Son. Each is Father and Son and Brother/Sister for the other. Each contributes to and benefits from the life and love of the other through the bond of the Spirit given to us).

Letting God be God means letting the Trinity be the Trinity. The members of the new covenant community participate in the Holy Spirit of the Father's and Son's covenant-creating and covenant-sustaining love to the extent that they allow (1) the Father's originating love in themselves and in others to originate that love, respectively, in others and in themselves, and (2) the Son in themselves and in others to welcome that love, respectively, from others and themselves. Mary and John are the historical counterparts in the community of covenant love to the Father and Son in the community of eternal love. Just as the love originating in the Father is eternally welcomed by the Son and shared in their Spirit, so the same Spirit is reflected as actively present and sustaining in the community of covenant love as the originating love of a mother and the originated love of a son. The Spirit of the Father and Son is known, in the biblical sense of knowing, in the giving and welcoming of their love within the covenant community, the matrix of Christian conversion as both an event and a life-long process. The Community of the Trinity's covenant love reflects the unrestricted love that is its life in its universal mission. The community of new covenant love manifests and proclaims that its God is a community of divine persons, a Triune God, summoning all humankind to communion and fulfillment in its eternal love. The love uniting the divine persons has been given to us in Jesus and his Spirit, summoning us to communion with each other in the same Spirit.

The universal story would be incomplete without my life story, a God-given gift to the universal story. At the same time, my/your story is meaningless apart from the God-given gift of the universal story. The authentic love that is given and received among persons within the universal story is the validating sign for Christian faith of the trinitarian love that is God's interpersonal life. To live and love in the Spirit of the Father and the Son is to know, within the limits of our human finitude, an authentic way of being and doing and seeing with others. It is a way of seeing God in all others, even in the darkness; for even loving our enemies falls within the scope of the gift of God's unrestricted and universal love. It is seeing God as he truly is (in love with all others) and others as they truly are (beloved of God) within the historical particularities of the universal story. All are lovable because God loves all and is with all (Emmanuel). The interpersonal relations of Father and Son and Spirit embrace all as their common origin, ground, direction, and destiny. The Christian community proclaims and celebrates the Good News that the Father has sent his Son and their Spirit to draw all forever into the fulness of their life and love. The kingdom of God is coming wherever persons are living the Spirit of God's originating and welcoming love.

4. REFLECTIONS ON GOSPEL LOVE

I. *Theological Reflection*

1. THE HAZARD OF SELF-DECEPTION

How do we know whether we truly love God and neighbor? Whether we truly adhere to the persons and values that we proclaim to be so dear to us? How do we know whether we are not the victims of our endless capacity for self-deception, suffering from illusions of moral and spiritual grandeur?

The New Testament writers express the Christian community's awareness of the danger of self-deception: "Let no one deceive himself: if any one of you thinks of himself as wise, in the ordinary sense of the word, then he must learn to be a fool before he really can be wise. Why? Because the wisdom of this world is foolishness to God" (1 Cor 3:18-19a) It is the people who are not important who often make the mistake of thinking that they are. "Let each of you examine his own conduct.... Everyone has his own burden to carry" (Gal 6:4-5). John also warns that our love "is not to be just words or mere talk, but something real" (1 Jn 3:18). How, then, do we tell the difference?

The structure of the Gospels, perhaps more than any particular text, expresses the Christian approach to both freedom *from* self-deception and freedom *for* an authentic communion with God in Jesus Christ and his community. All four Gospels center on the passion narrative (Mk 14—15; Mt 26—27; Lk 22—23; Jn 18—19). The passion is proclaimed, not merely narrated; it is the central saving event in the history of salvation, the climax and fulfillment of the saving and judging acts of God. Hence there are numerous allusions to the fulfillment of the Old Testament in the passion; it is the event which Jesus himself presents as the goal and fulfillment of his life and mission. Jesus voluntarily accepts suffering and death out of love for his Father and all human persons. This is Good News not only of God's unconditional love for us, but also of the way for ascertaining the authenticity of our commitment to God and all others.[1] Jesus Christ not only enables us to share his authentic communion with God, but he also liberates us from self-deception about the reality of our love for God and others.

2. THE AUTHORITY OF LOVE

Christian faith does not question God's love for us; it does question the authenticity of our love for God. The crucified and risen Jesus Christ defines how Christians understand both the grace and demand of God's love for us. Jesus Christ defines the meaning of authentic communion with God. He possesses it; therefore, he can communicate it. He is the Authority, for Christians, who authors our authentic communion with God. He taught with authority (Mk 1:22), not as the scribes appealing elsewhere; not as the prophets, declaring: "Thus says the Lord," but with authority: "I say to you..." (Mt 5:22,28,32,34, 39, 44). He claimed that all authority was his (Mt 28:18; Jn 17:2), and he gave his

---

[1] The pseudo-discipleship of those claiming communion with the Lord without having followed his way of the cross seems to be the form of self-deception involved in *Matthew* 7:21-23: "On that day many will say to me, 'Lord, Lord, did we not prophesy in your name, and cast out demons in your name, and do many mighty works in your name?'... And then I will say to them, 'I never knew you; depart from me, you evildoers'" Affirming that Jesus is our Lord on the basis of having received his gifts does not suffice for true discipleship.

followers the right they did not otherwise possess: to become sons of God (Jn 1:12). God can do as he will; his authority is absolute; and he has manifested and communicated his authority in Jesus Christ for the coming of his kingdom in love. The authority of Jesus Christ is that of his being-in-Love, which reveals that "God is Love" (1 Jn 4:8, 16). He summons all to become children of God by accepting and participating in his dynamic state of being-in-Love.[2]

Being-in-Love (the mutual indwelling of the Father and the Son in their Spirit), inviting our becoming sons and daughters in the Son, entails our accepting a relationship to the Love that transcends every merely human love. We do not establish that relationship; it is given to us. We do not possess it by nature; therefore, it cannot be taken for granted.[3] We can fail to accept the gift of God's love and his call to become sons in the Son. Self-deception is one way: we can assume that we are authentically in communion with God in Jesus Christ, without following his way of the cross. We can assume that we share his being-in-Love without undergoing the suffering that is entailed in his meeting the demands and total claims of Love. Suffering in meeting these demands and claims is evidence of our having authentically accepted the gift of God's love, of our fulfilling God's will rather than our independent will. The passion narrative presents the fulfillment of God's will, paradigmatically, in the sufferings of the Just One. The sovereignty of God's love, as opposed to self-love, is manifested in the sufferings of the just.

---

[2] See Bernard Lonergan, *Method in Theology* (London: Darton, Longmans & Todd, 1971) with regard to the state of being in love (pp. 33, 105, 106, 109, 113, 119, 122, 240, 283, 289). Christian scriptures symbolize the realm of transcendent and unrestricted Love in Trinitarian imagery which interprets that realm in interpersonal terms. Jesus Christ's being-in-Love derives from his interpersonal relations with his Father and Spirit. The New Testament points to Jesus as the revelation of the Father who completes his mission by sending the Spirit.

[3] Charles Hefling affirms that the gift of God's love flooding our hearts is the gracious gift of a conversion; that it is not a gift that can be taken for granted, as though it were a secure and permanent possession; that religious authenticity, therefore, has to be cultivated by instruction and self-denial, examination of conscience, and prayer. See his Introduction to Frederick E. Crowe, *The Lonergan Enterprise* (Cambridge, MA: Cowley Publications, 1980), p. xvi.

3. THE POWER OF LOVE

The Synoptics present their story of Jesus in four phases with the implication that he has established a new people who in faith and trust continue his mission, following him on the way of the cross, and have his life-in-Love: (1) preparation (Mt 3:1—4:11 = Mk 1:1-13 = Lk 3:1—4:13); (2) the ministry in Galilee (Mt 4:12—18:35 = Mk 1:14—9:50 = Lk 4:14—9:50); (3) the journey to Jerusalem (Mt 19:1—20:34 = Mk 10:1-52 = Lk 9:51—18:43); (4) the passion and resurrection (Mt 21—28 = Mk 11—16 = Lk 19—24). The Gospel writers want their readers to be transformed by authentically sharing Jesus Christ's life and his Spirit in the process of dying and rising with him. This is the structure of the life of Jesus, and the structure of the lives of all who are baptized into him, into his death and resurrection. His suffering and death must not only be proclaimed, but also shared. The life that is shared in faith and through the Spirit is the *whole* life of Jesus, his dying and his rising, his self-emptying and his glorification, his being-in-Love. The power that Jesus exercised when his life reached its climax in the decisive moments of his passion and death was the power of his being-in-Love, the power of his life over death itself. The mystery of cross and resurrection expresses the true nature and power of Jesus' being-in-Love, the power of being able to love "unto the end," and to lay down his life for his friends.

Jesus anticipated his passion and death; he found in it the deep mystery of God's saving will on behalf of "many" (a Semitic expression [Is 53:12] for "everyone"). Jesus thrice forecast to his disciples his suffering, death, and resurrection ([a] Mk 8:31-32 = Mt 16:21 = Lk 9:22; [b] Mk 9:31-32 = Mt 17:21-23 = Lk 9:43-45; [c] Mk 10:32-34 = Mt 20:17-19 = Lk 18:31-34). After the Transfiguration he taught that the Son of man must suffer many things (Mk 9:12 = Mt 17:12; cf. Lk 17:25). The disciple who shares his Lord's destiny will also be called upon to suffer. Jesus tells his followers that they must expect suffering and rejection and persecution (Mk 8:34-35; Mt 10:24-25; Lk 6:22 and 14:26-27; Jn 12:23-26). To share his vision and mission in the service of the kingdom is to suffer with him. Discipleship is the gift of God's love which makes it possible for a person to follow Jesus and renounce those things which seem ultimate in life: "Whoever loses his life for my sake and the gospel's will save it" (Mk 8:35). Jesus' demand is actually an invitation to new life in the Spirit uniting him to his Father, with the implication that this is the only life which really counts. His call, "follow me" (Mk 1:17) is a command which implies his total claim to our self-renunciation on behalf of the kingdom. To deny or reject him is to refuse the dominion of God and his rule in love because one prefers one's autonomy, self-rule, and illusory self-sufficiency. To be with Jesus Christ is to be with one who exists only for Another, who is-in-Love and for-Love; consequently, the authentic disciple denies himself and takes up his cross to meet the total claims of Love with the invincible power that derives from his Father's Spirit.

4. FROM COMPASSION TO PASSION

In the Gospel stories we see the link between the compassion of Jesus and his passion.[4] The active compassion of Jesus reaches out to the sick, the hungry, the blind, the lame, the possessed, the sinner. His compassion is a sign of the kingdom, of his being and living in the Spirit of his Father's love for him and all others. His compassion is an affirmation of good over evil and of life over death. Mark tells of Jesus feeding the multitude because he had "compassion" on them (8:2), and then he tells of Jesus giving sight to the blind man of Bethsaida (8:22-26), and finally he says that Jesus began to teach them that he had to "suffer many things," and even be put to death (8:31). The compassion of Jesus or his "suffering with" reaches its culmination in his passion, his "suffering for." In his compassion he moved to his passion, which John portrays as his loving "unto the end" (13:1). The compassion of Jesus becomes his passion as

---

[4]I am indebted to William V. Dych for his spelling out the link between the compassion and passion in his unpublished manuscript, *Through A Glass Darkly*, (no date given).

the final and ultimate sign of his being-in-Love. The passion is the culmination, or final moment, of his compassion. The sign of the kingdom's coming is realized when compassion with others leads to passion for others: "'A man can have no greater love than to lay down his life for his friends'" (Jn 15:13). Compassion must become passion for the disciple as well as for the master, for this is the ultimate measure of our being-in-Love, in the Spirit that is the life of mutual indwelling of Father and Son.

5. THE QUICKSANDS OF SELF-SUFFICIENCY

Jesus saw the ambiguity of the human heart, its goodness and evil, for "he knew what was in man" (Jn 2:25). His vision of the kingdom was one in which that heart could be transformed with new life, the life that he and his Father share in their Spirit. Jesus saw the "imperfect" and "unfinished" character of a world of good and evil, a world intent on its self-glorification, a world with illusions of self-sufficiency. This world could be redeemed and transformed by and in the Spirit of his Father's love for him and all others, the Spirit of his love for his Father and all others. Through the gift of that Spirit all things could be made new. The life and ministry of Jesus that is portrayed in the New Testament is in the service of his Father's will to communicate the rule of his love through and in the gift of their Spirit of mutual indwelling love. Jesus lives and dies and rises to communicate that redeeming and transforming Spirit of his filial love for his Father, the same Spirit of his Father's love for all in his Beloved Son. His service of compassion manifests the Spirit of the Lord that is upon him, effecting the hoped-for deliverance of an "imperfect" and "unfinished" world (Lk 4:18), a world in need of the kingdom for its true fulfillment.

6. "IF YOU KNOW THESE THINGS"

When Jesus takes the role of the servant washing the feet of his disciples at the last supper, he tells them that his role is paradigmatic of their own relationship to one another and to the kingdom: "'If I, then, your Lord and Master, have washed your feet, you also ought to wash one another's feet. For I have given you an example, that you also should do as I have done'" (Jn 13:14-15). His service is the sign of his living in the Spirit that is both his life/love given to the Father and his Father's life/love given to him. His service is in giving that life for all so that all human relationships be transformed by and in the Spirit that unites Father and Son in mutual indwelling love. The kingdom is coming where human persons welcome and serve each other in that Spirit. The final words of this last supper scene are his call to sharing his service: "'If you know these things, blessed are you if you do them'" (Jn 13:17). Discipleship means living in that Spirit that is making all things new in the transforming power of the same reciprocal and universal love that is the life of Jesus and his Father.

7. FREEDOM—ENABLING GRACE

Matthew's story of the Last Judgment (25:31-46) teaches that the kingdom comes with total claims upon every person. To ignore these claims is to reject them. The righteous are those whom the Son of Man will declare to have, in truth, done the will of God (25:37, 46). They have lived according to the definite claims of the kingdom for solidarity with the Son of Man in serving God and his kingdom. The measure of their compassion for others is the measure of their solidarity and service. Those who lacked compassion did not thereby deny the kingdom to others, but they lost the kingdom for themselves. The grace and demand of new life in the kingdom confronts our freedom in the person of Jesus Christ. Our freedom to accept or reject this new life is dependent on the grace that is Jesus Christ. We have nothing that we have not received, and we cannot love unless we have been loved, we cannot be compassionate unless we have received compassion. Because God has given us *his* love and compassion in Jesus Christ, we are free to respond (response-able) with his love and compassion for others. We are responsible to the Son of Man for others.

The ultimate principle and source of our knowledge of

God is the being-in-Love that is the life of the Son in the Father, given to us in the Holy Spirit, which is our power to bear all things, believe all things, hope all things, endure all things (1 Cor 13:7). The whole person knows God in the lived-knowledge of faith and hope and love.

Like the Evangelists, Paul also speaks of knowing God. In Paul's epistemology, such knowledge is not exempted from the law of the cross, the law of love. Paul tells the Corinthians that he "knows nothing except Jesus Christ, and him crucified" (1 Cor 2:2). Such knowledge is knowledge through connaturality. For it is through Paul's dying and rising in the Spirit of Jesus Christ that he shares his being-in-Love. Paul speaks of such knowledge as a "being known." He tells the Galatians that they are free because they "are known by God" (4:9). Knowledge of God, then, is not a grasping or mastering or comprehending, but a being grasped and being known and loved. The truth of Paul's trust makes him free to affirm that "I shall know fully even as I am fully known" (1 Cor 13:12).

8. STRUGGLE AND RESISTANCE

The kingdom of God that comes to us in the mystery of Jesus Christ's dying and rising is a sign of contradiction. Fidelity to the Master means that the disciple must enter into the same struggle that he entered to fulfill God's plan for creation. Opposition to Jesus is manifested within all his human contexts. Society, family, and even his followers fail to grasp his vision and resist his mission on behalf of the kingdom. Mark structures his Gospel to underscore human resistance to the arrival of the kingdom in the person, work and ministry, of Jesus Christ.[5] Society (the people) resists

---

[5]Xavier Leon-Dufour's interpretation of Mark's structure is used, with a slight modification (i.e. the extension of the section, "Jesus and his disciples," from 8:30 to 8:33). The first half of the Gospel ("The Mystery of the Messiah") is divided into three sections in which Jesus confronts respectively, his people and family and disciples. Leon-Dufour's interpretation is found in his book, *introduzione al nuovo testamento* Augustin George and Pierre Grelot, Eds., Vol. 2, *L'annuncio del vangelo*, trans. from French by A. Mastrandrea and B. Liverani, (Roma: Borla, 1976), p. 46.

Jesus (1:14—3:6). The Pharisees and scribes, leaders of the people, engage him in five controversies (2:1—3:5) and decide to destroy him (3:6). His family, relatives and townspeople are disturbed by him (3:7—6:6). They attempt to seize him because they believe that he is out of his mind (3:21). He is despised in his own country, among his own relations and in his own house (6:4) He is amazed at their lack of faith (6:6); he could work no miracle there. Jesus meets with the incomprehension of his own disciples (6:6—8:33). He rebukes them for not understanding the miracle of the loaves (8:17) and the necessity of his passion and death (8:31). He sharply rebukes Peter: "Get behind me, Satan! For you are not on the side of God, but of men" (8:33). Fidelity to the will of God meets with human resistance and incomprehension. The kingdom of God is not ours by nature. If it were, Jesus would not encounter incomprehension, hostility, rejection.[6] His harmony with the will of God entails his disharmony with all that is opposed to it. His being-in-Love entails his suffering and death out of love that all persons might be-in-Love. He loves his people, family, disciples, and all others with whom his life and vision and mission are in conflict; he suffers out of love for them with the compassion that leads to his passion and death, in order that all might have the fullness of new life in the kingdom.[7]

---

[6] A list of the enemies of Jesus for the entire Gospel of Mark is given in Paul Winter's *On the Trial of Jesus* ("Studia Judaica," 1 [Berlin: de Gruyter, 1961]), pp. 121-123, 343, n.20.

The opponents who speak against Jesus in the conflict stories during the Jerusalem ministry (Mark 11-12, and par.) may be listed in terms of those to whom he says "No": (1) the Zealots and their wishes (Mk 12: 13-17); (2) the Sadducees and their hypocrisy (Mk 12:18-27); (3) the Pharisees and their legalism (Mk 12:28-34). Chief priests, scribes, and elders clash with Jesus on the question about his divine authority (11:27).

See J.C. Weber, Jr., "Jesus' Opponents in the Gospel of Mark," *The Journal of Bible and Religion*, 34 (1966), 214-22. Also John Reumann, *Jesus in the Church's Gospels* (Philadelphia: Fortress Press, 1968) 251-60, 416-17.

[7] The Gospels contrast the suffering service of Jesus with the smug self-righteousness of Israel's religious leaders, implying that authentically religious persons are those who follow Jesus' way of self-sacrifice for others with a love that is rooted in God. Jesus' fidelity to God brings him into conflict with others; his progressive fulfillment of God's will is commensurate with his loss of human approval. He warns his disciples: "'If they persecuted me, they will persecute you

As God's will for him is being progressively fulfilled, Jesus becomes increasingly unpopular until he dies alone, rejected and abandoned by all. Thus, Mark's narrative structure makes the theological point that God alone is the fulfilling origin and ground and destiny of Jesus Christ's living and dying and rising out of love. The coming of the kingdom in the person of Jesus Christ is the revelation that God is in love with all human persons and summons them to be and to become in his love his new creation. What is demanded of us is repentance and faith (Mk 1:15) in his love given to us in his Beloved Son (Mk 1:11; 9:7). Such repentance and faith entails the suffering out of love which the Beloved Son himself experienced in his prayer at Gethsemane (Mk 14:36). Jesus experiences suffering out of love in every human context, the intrapersonal as well as the interpersonal; it is evidence that the integrating center of his life transcends every human context. God's lordship in love is a creative goodness which *makes* others good. When God begins his reign as Father in Jesus Christ, all things are made new in his love, all things are possible (Mk 10:27; 14:36; Mt. 19:26; Lk 18:27).

9. TOTAL CLAIMS OF THE KINGDOM

The structure of Mark's narrative is theologically illuminating with regard to the tensions, suffering, conflicts, and death that accompany the gift of new life-in-Love that is revealed in Jesus Christ's fulfillment of his Father's will. The new life that is given to all in Jesus Christ unsettles or challenges everyone (society, family, friends and disciples); it does not endear him to everyone. Jesus' life-and-death-in-Love creates bewilderment and disorientation within every human context. His life, rooted in a disconcerting Love, is a new life that does not leave old life in peace; it *demands* the transformation of all his human contexts at both the intrapersonal and interpersonal levels. Jesus is a suffering sign of

---

too...'" (Jn 15:20). Such persecution is linked with seeking God's glory or doing his will: "'If I were to seek my own glory that would be no glory at all; my glory is conferred by the Father....I faithfully keep his word'" (Jn 8:55).

contradiction because he loves all the persons within his various human contexts, despite their resistance or rejection; he is the personal form of God's love that would, despite themselves, *make* them all truly good persons.

In Jesus Christ's suffering out-of-love, the Christian community sees that he is-in-Love; that God compassionately and passionately demands that all persons find and accept their true fulfillment in the gift of his love; that all might become and forever be persons-in-Love through the gift of his love that is Jesus Christ and his Spirit; that God is not indifferent to what we are and become; that the failure to accept his love for all is the failure to become and to be forever an authentic person-in-Love; that to accept his love for all is to learn to suffer with His compassionate and passionate love for all, overcoming our intrapersonal and interpersonal tendencies to remain impersonal.

10. "HAPPY TO SUFFER FOR YOU"

The new life of the kingdom that is given to us in Jesus Christ and his Spirit entails the suffering out-of-Love for others that manifests our being-in-Love for others. This new life transforms us by making us willing and glad to suffer for others in the service of the kingdom. In the context of the last supper, John's Gospel implies that Jesus gladly and voluntarily lays down his life that his friends might know the joy of being able to do likewise: "'... that my own joy may be in you and your joy may be complete'" (15:11).

Paul's authentic discipleship is reflected in his being glad to suffer out of love for others: "It makes me happy to suffer for you, as I am suffering now, and in my own body to do what I can to make up all that has still to be undergone by Christ for the sake of his body, the Church" (Col 1: 24). The true disciple loves as his master loves. They share a life that is rooted in God's community-creating love for all, the only love that constitutes the community of divine and human persons which lasts forever. They have solidarity in that invincible love which, despite suffering and death itself, makes them glad to pour out their lives for others. They do not consider themselves to be martyrs or victims; rather, they gladly suffer for others (divine and human) as true friends in the power of that love which alone grounds the eternal friendship that is life in the kingdom.

11. "THE JOY THAT NO ONE SHALL TAKE FROM YOU"

Central to the notion of Christian conversion as suffering out of love is the fact that God wants all human persons to enjoy his life as their own. The gift of God's love is not so much a giving away as sharing. God shares Himself, all that He is and cherishes and enjoys, in his loving of human beings. Jesus Christ *joys* in the life and love of his Father; therefore, he is *glad* to suffer out of that love so that all human beings might share what he most cherishes. The life which he so gladly receives as the Beloved Son is the life he so gladly communicates in his suffering out of love for others. On the eve of his death, he consoles his disciples with the reason that he is glad to give up his life for them: ". . . I shall see you again, and your hearts will be full of joy, and that joy no one shall take from you" (Jn 16:22). In the same context, Jesus prays to his Father for his disciples: "I say these things to share my joy with them to the full" (Jn 17:13). The joy of Jesus becomes the joy of the disciple: "What we have seen and heard we are telling you so that you too may be in union with us, as we are in union with the Father and with his Son Jesus Christ. We are writing this to you to make our own joy complete" (1 Jn 1:4). The joy that Jesus promised and bestowed upon his disciples comes from fellowship with the Father (cf. Jn 15:10-11) and finds its constant fulfillment in their ministry (of which John's letter is a part).

What is perfect in the Master is imperfect in the disciple. The life that Jesus Christ fully enjoys is the life that his disciples are learning to enjoy. The disciple knows (in the biblical sense) the Master to the extent that he or she enjoys the same life and is glad to suffer out of love to secure that life for others. The solidarity of Master and disciple in suffering out of love for others consists in their enjoyment /cherishing of the life that they want others to enjoy. Christian conversion is not only an event but also a process in which this solidarity is deepened through fidelity to the grace and demand of God for responsible lives.

12. BEFRIENDING LOVE

Christian conversion, both as event and process, is participation in the befriending love which Jesus Christ received and accepted from his Father as the integrating center of his life and mission and death for others. Titus is told that in sending his Son among us, God has shown himself the "friend of humankind" (Tit 3:4). As the agent of his Father's befriending love, Jesus tells his disciples at the last supper: "'I no longer call you servants, but friends'" (Jn 15:15). His suffering out of the love with which his Father befriends all in his kingdom is shared by his friends (disciples): "'You are the men who have stood faithfully by me in my trials; and now I confer a kingdom on you, just as my Father conferred one on me'" (Lk 22: 28-29). His compassion and passion are the work of his Father's befriending love, a love which knows no limit or exception: "When we were reconciled to God by the death of his Son, we were still enemies..." (Rom 5:11).

Christian conversion, as lived, entails suffering out of a befriending love that affects all our conscious activities, directs our attention, pervades our imagination, releases symbols that penetrate to the depths of our psyche, enriches our understanding, guides our judgments, reinforces our decisions, and motivates our actions. To enjoy the transforming benefit of God's befriending love in Jesus Christ and his Spirit implies the gratitude that actively accepts it and willingly pays the price in religious and moral commitment that others share it. Gratitude for the gift of God's befriending love reflects the humility that takes nothing for granted. Such humility brings an appreciation of and commitment to others, even when they are superficially unattractive.⁸ If we accept the world and our own existence with religious gratitude, that does not mean passivity. If they are good, they deserve to be improved. They call for the basic commitment which, like appreciation, takes nothing for granted. If we truly appreciate others, we are glad to suffer out of love for them, to befriend them, as disciples of the Master who lived and died to make his joy ours.

The Gospels are the Church's pedagogical resource for promoting Christian conversion, both as event and as a process of maturation. The Gospel writers highlight the compassion and passion of Jesus with the implication that the authenticity of our response to his injunction to love God above all else finds its measure in the deeds by which we follow him in self-sacrificing and befriending love for others. ⁹ The transforming power of Jesus' acceptance of death out of love for others implies that wherever our activity flows from an authentically self-sacrificing and befriending love, the conversion process is occurring. Faith in the reality of the befriending God revealed in the compassion and passion of Jesus underpins the dynamism of charity and hope in self-sacrifice for others. The Gospels are written for the communication and cultivation of this faith, hope, and charity. They express the Christian community's conviction that God alone fulfills our "unfinished" world through and in the gift of his Spirit, the mutual and indwelling love of the Father and Son that is the origin, direction, ground and destiny of all human life.

---

⁸See Bartholomew Kiely, *Psychology and Moral Theology* (Rome: Gregorian University Press, 1980), pp. 227-31.

⁹John's Gospel presents Love as the reason for the incarnation: "For God so loved the world that he gave his only Son, that whoever believes in him should not perish but have eternal life. for, God sent the Son into the world, not to condemn the world, but that the world might be saved through him"(3:16-17). The crucifixion is *the* symbol of self-sacrificing love. The reality behind that symbol makes it possible for Christians to live in a community whose sign to the world is their love for one another after the example of the Word who revealed the Father's love for humankind. Jesus' community is to be known to all because it continues the self-sacrificing love of Jesus (13:34-35; 15:9-13).

II. Principles and Practical Points of Reference

1. Being-in-Love is the motivating power for suffering out-of-Love.

2. If God is (as Jesus Christ reveals) befriending-Love, being-in-befriending-Love is the motivating power for suffering out-of-befriending-Love for others. It makes us glad, despite difficulties, to befriend others.

3. Suffering out-of-befriending-Love for others is the self-transcending activity that frees us *from* self-absorption, self-pity, and self-idolatry (i.e. from being impersonal); it frees us *for* the fulfillment that is being-in-love with others (i.e. for being personal).

4. For human beings to be fully personal is, ultimately, for them to be-in-Love-befriending-others. Sin is the refusal to be personal, the state of the impersonal subject.

5. In Christian conversion, as lived, suffering is not sought for its own sake; rather, it is embraced only when it is a condition for commitment to the grace and demand of God's befriending love.

6. If Christian conversion, as lived, entails suffering out-of-befriending-Love for others, suffering is not a univocal sign that something is wrong with a person; it may be, as the teaching of the beatitudes implies, the sign that something is profoundly right with a person.

7. We are not committed to persons (or values) for whom we are unwilling to suffer. We cannot give what we do not have. *Nemo dat quod non habet.* We cannot suffer out of love for others, when we have no love for them.

8. The being-in-Love that is Christian conversion, as lived, is the efficacious ground of the self-transcendence that is required to live responsibly and to be responsible in the pursuit of the truth, however difficult it may be to discover or to accept the truth. It motivates the will to be responsible and to pay the price of responsibility.

9. The fact that Jesus Christ was willing and glad to suffer and die for us grounds the primary dogma that God loves us. To sense that we are loved is therefore to sense something that is true. It may well be that imagination is involved in our sensation, but nevertheless the truth of the dogma must stand. The mistake is to identify the love with the sensation, so that the cessation of the feeling is taken to mean the cessation of the love. Similarly, the determination and gladness of Jesus in embracing suffering out of love should not be identified with mere pleasure or feeling or sensation. Being-in-Love and being determined and glad to suffer out of love for others should never be identified with any particular kind of feeling or sensation. Our faith and hope is in God, not in our feelings: we do not suffer out of love for our feelings.

10. Because human beings are limited and leave something to be desired that God alone can fulfill, suffering out of love is the condition for the possibility of friendship. Friendship (marriage, community, society, etc.) disintegrates with the refusal to endure limitations and deficiencies in others. Our incapacity for friendship (marriage, etc.) is related to our unwillingness to be committed to others who do not fully gratify, support, or console us. One happily married individual commented: "There is no marriage so perfect that a spouse could not find a motive for a divorce, should he or she be looking for one." There is no lasting commitment to others apart from the willingness to suffer out of love for them.

11. Having time for others is a form of suffering out of love for them. Religious conversion implies that we are living in God's time, that we have the gift of his time for welcoming and listening to others; consequently, we do not see others as taking or consuming *our* time, and we are free for them to the extent that we are free from the illusion that the only time we have is our own. Being-in-

Love might be interpreted as being in God's time, as having his time for patiently befriending and encouraging others through the gift of a love whose power endures forever. Prayer is a form of enjoying God's time and of transcending our own. Some seldom find time to pray because they are living in their own time and do not want to lose it for life in God's time. Ironically, they know that their time is limited or running out. Prayer is learning to live in God's time with the patient love that befriends all in the kingdom. The call to pray always is the call to be-in-Love and to live in God's time forever.

12. Suffering out of love for others is a form of our self-investment in them. Through such suffering we bear a word of faith and hope for them. Inasmuch as communities are formed and held together by a common faith and hope, there is a community-creating and community-sustaining power and value in suffering out of faith and hope and love for others. The crucified and risen Jesus is God's loving self-investment in every human life for the coming of his kingdom. The compassion and passion of Jesus reveals God's making a gift of new possibilities for life under the sovereignty of his love in the kingdom.

13. Inconveniencing ourselves for others is perhaps the most basic and common form of suffering out of love for others. The unwillingness to inconvenience ourselves for others is the refusal to be personal; it is the failure to befriend others at the most rudimentary level of everyday life with others. There is no possibility of a lasting commitment to others without our being willing to inconvenience ourselves for them daily. Martyrdom is the heroic, dramatic, single-day expression of the no less heroic, undramatic, everyday suffering out of love for others that is at the heart of Christian living. If our notions of suffering out of love for others have no sober anchorage in the concrete realities of everyday life, we shall be tempted to despise the most rudimentary

demands of Christian charity in favor of religious experience that is an evasion of reality. The rhetoric of sweeping generalizations often betrays the illusions of spiritual grandeur in persons who despise the everyday demands of concrete others for their befriending love. The massiveness of our ambitions can represent our pathological flight from having to inconvenience ourselves for ordinary others.

14. The New Testament demand for human transformation through following Jesus' way of the cross should warn those who are tempted to reduce God to their own measure. The self-abandonment that God's befriending love required of Jesus Christ should correct our tendency to manipulate God for self-apotheosis.

15. To the extent that I am convinced that my importance is in God, as opposed to the illusion of an independent self-importance, I am equally convinced that all others have the same importance and are worthy of my self-sacrificing and befriending love. The conviction that I am because God loves me implies that I find my security and sense of personal worth in God, rather than in the approval that others may choose to give me. If we can accept ourselves as the gift of an incomprehensible love, we are free to recognize others as such and to pay the price of commitment to them. God alone gives us that invincible security with regard to our importance and worth, without which we implicitly despise ourselves and all those who need such a "despicable" self. Self-importance reflects the radical insecurity of those who seek to be important for those who do not need them, while rejecting those for whom they are truly important.

16. If God's will is done, all human persons will be in his kingdom. Letting God be God consists in accepting the sovereignty of his love, the coming of the kingdom of his love. God alone actually loves all persons. Our finite, limited, human love is inadequate to the chal-

lenge of loving all persons, apart from the gift of God's all-embracing, all-encompassing, all-sustaining, all-forgiving, all-reconciling, and all-fulfilling love. His community-creating love for all is the origin and ground of life in the kingdom.

17. Love takes others seriously. How seriously we take others, according to the Judeo-Christian tradition, reflects how seriously we take God. That God takes all persons seriously is the conviction of this tradition. Christians affirm that God is Love because he sent his only Son in freedom and love to live and die for us. The Love that is Ultimate Reality, as opposed to "just words or mere talk" (1 Jn 3:18), has embraced human living and suffering and dying. We know that we are truly loved or taken seriously by those who, despite all, gladly and willingly share our living and suffering and dying. Similarly, we discover the reality of our love for others (human and divine) in our gladly and willingly doing likewise. The cross, therefore, reveals the truth of God's love for us and verifies our love for one another. The cross is the measure of our commitment in freedom and love to all others.

5. WHY WE SHARE THE GOOD NEWS: *LEX NARRANDI, LEX CREDENDI*

The imperative of covenant love to share the Spirit of Jesus Christ and his Father that all humankind may see the salvation of God (Is 40:5 = Lk 3:6) motivates the Christian community's communicating the Good News.

The friends of God in the Judeo-Christian tradition are united as the community that remembers to share and to celebrate the life that God has given to them. Theirs is the faith and hope that lives in remembering to tell the story of God's steadfast covenant love, the origin and ground and destiny of their life as a people. Being in love with God means remembering to share the gift of his love by telling and celebrating our story of its goodness. Telling the story is at the heart of the community's life of faith and worship; it is the *lex narrandi*, a governing principle like that of the *lex orandi* and *lex credendi*, which is constitutive of the community's existence and purpose. Telling the story is one of the ways in which the gift of God's love is operative in the imagination and memory and anticipation of the community of faith.

Moses recounts the wonderful deeds of God for the people that he has chosen as his own. He warns his people never to forget them (Dt 6:10-13). Remembering to tell their story of God and his saving goodness is an obligation of the children of Abraham: "Remember how Yahweh your God..." (Dt 8:2). Remembering is for learning: "Learn from this that Yahweh your God was training you as a man trains his child..." (Dt 8:5). Remembering to tell the story encourages hope: "Remember Yahweh your God: it was he who gave you this strength and won you this power..."(Dt 8:18). Remembering is a collective activity that unites the community of faith. To forget their story of God, their common heritage, entails their destruction as a people: "Be sure that if you forget Yahweh your God...you will most certainly perish" (Dt 8:19). Israel lives in sharing and communicating its story of God.

Israel tells its story of God in its prayers. The *lex narrandi* cannot be separated from the *lex orandi*; for knowing God in the Hebrew sense arises from lived experience, requiring that the person is possessed by Yahweh, acknowledges in mind and heart God's sovereignty, and lives a loving response by doing God's will. The Psalmist reaffirms the *lex narrandi* as the obligation of covenant love to communicate the story of God's compassionate deeds for the benefit of future generations:

> Listen to this Law, my people....
> What we have heard and known for ourselves,
> and what our ancestors have told us,
> must not be withheld from their descendants,
> but handed on by us to the next generation,
> that is: the titles of God, his power
> and the miracles he has done.
> When he issued the decrees for Jacob
> and instituted a Law in Israel,
> he gave our ancestors strict orders
> to teach it to their children;
> the next generation was to learn it,

and children still to be born,
and these in their turn were to tell their own children
so that they too would put their confidence in God,
never forgetting God's achievements,
and always keeping his commandments (Ps 78: 177)

The Psalmist reminds the community of faith that just as their ancestors had heard the word of God in their own lives and had kept it for them, they too must communicate that same word of hope for future generations. Their lives of faith and hope are interwoven with those of their ancestors and of future generations. Through their ancestors, who remembered to share and to communicate their story of God, the present generation has been prepared to recognize and to experience the true goodness of God within the unique historical particularities of their life story. The Psalm, or prayer, of the community is one hope for future generations. It expresses responsible love for the past and present and future of the community that God is creating and sustaining. The prayerful telling of the story reflects the mature love of the friends of God in their accepting responsibility for the life of the community. Their remembering expresses and communicates their love for others. Their storytelling bears a word of hope that others might have life more fully.

Both Moses and the Psalmist, representing the law and the prayer of Israel, share the vision of a universal story under a God who is actively encompassing their lives within the goodness of his own. Both accept responsibility for remembering to share their story of God's saving deeds; both enjoin the community of faith to accept the grace and demand of covenant love for telling the same story for the life of the people that God is calling into existence in every age. Both summon the community to tell of the God who is present here and now, not separate and distant in his own world; of the God who is alive and enlivening and is in his own place in the life of the community; of the God whose presence is not silent, but communicating as he creates and sustains his people, summoning them to give themselves in covenant love and to be with him in doing what he is doing for others.

Israel's authentic listening and telling expresses God's speaking and acting within its historical experience. The *Shema*, the prayer that is Israel's confession of faith, shares the concern of Moses and the Psalmist for authentic listening with its injunction, "Listen, O Israel!" (Dt 5:4); for there is no life story for Israel to remember and to communicate as a word of hope for others apart from its docile listening to God's gracious word calling for decision and action. Learning to listen within our own life story for the community-creating and community-sustaining grace and demand of God for responsible living is at the heart of Israel's religious pedagogy. The word of God is to be heard and to be put into practice at intrapersonal and interpersonal and social levels of the covenant community's life.

Our listening and telling relationship to God's speaking and acting constitutes our life and identity as a covenant people. Only a people that hears God's, "I love you" (Jer 31:2; Mal 1:2) can reply "Love God, all you devout" (Ps 31:24; Ps 97:10), in its common commitment to its Lover, and affirm "I am his" (Sg 2:16). Our lived faith experience that God is caring for us as a people grounds our conviction that we are responsible to God for our lives as a people. We know in the events of our life as a people a caring God who is summoning us to be with him in caring for ourselves and one another as a people. Because we have life as belonging to a people, we are being truly responsible to God for ourselves as individuals only when we are being coresponsible to him for the people through and in whom we live. God is truly served by those who serve his people. The psalmist concludes by recalling David as a model of such service:

> "Choosing David as his servant....
> to pasture his people Jacob and Israel his heritage:
> who did this with unselfish care
> and led them with a sensitive hand" (Ps 78:70,72)

Israel confessed her faith characteristically by recounting

the story of her life: "We were once slaves of the mightiest emperor of the day, but Yahweh, the God of our fathers, brought us up out of Egypt and led us into a good and broad land." Israel began her confession of faith by pointing to the historical situation of distress and limitation from which, in a wholly unexpected and humanly impossible way, deliverance was granted. In that situation, the Exodus from Egypt, the reality of God was unveiled. What we mean by God, Israel declares, is this Reality who opened a way into the future when there was no way. This is the Reality whom we have encountered in our history and who with boundless compassion deals with us in the concrete situations of our historical journey. This God, whose name is Yahweh, is not remote and inaccessible; he is the God who makes himself present, who is "with us" (Immanuel). As the prophet Hosea put it, he is "the Holy One in your midst" (Hos 11:9). Whether his coming to his people is experienced as judgment or mercy, the saving effect is the same: he opens a way into the future when no way exists. He gives his people a new possibility — in grace. He inspires confidence:

> O Israel, hope in Yahweh.
> For with Yahweh there is steadfast love,
> and with him is plenteous redemption (Ps 130:7).

One of the basic differences between Israel's psalms and the songs of her neighbors is that Israel turned primarily to her own historical experience to proclaim the reality of God to the world. Israel affirms that God's people was created out of the nothingness of historical oblivion, the chaos of meaningless oppression. Therefore, Yahweh is praised as Israel's maker: "let us kneel before Yahweh, our maker!" (Ps 95:6).

In Israel's great festivals the story of the formation of the people was told and retold as a drama in which the present generation was involved. The worshippers acknowledged that the whole story had happened for them. They were participants in the Exodus story; they recognized its meaning for the here and now. Accordingly, the faithful Israelite confessed that "Yahweh delivered *us* from Egypt, guided *us* through the great and terrible wilderness, and led *us* into the land of the new beginning." The Passover guests did not start to eat until the Passover *haggahdah* had been said. The *haggahdah*, or "narrative", was the Passover story and it was a recital of the great events of the redemption as these were suggested by the symbolism employed by the meal.

Even today the Passover ritual contains the reminder that the believing Jews should confess that the Lord brought *them* out of Egypt. In the Christian community the believer also confesses that the whole story, which comes to its completion in Jesus Christ, has happened "for me" and "for us." The community of faith has a shared history. It confesses its faith by retelling its story of God's action with his people in the history of Israel because it believes that the same God is operative with the same saving purpose in the historical particularities of our lives here and now (*lex credendi*). The community of faith "knows God," in the biblical sense, in its life story. It attributes that story to the mercy of God and praises him for it. Telling the story is a form of public confession with praise and adoration, a testimony to God's goodness. At daily worship it is heard as a summons to ongoing commitment to believe and hope and obey and serve him with loving gratitude.

Israel's psalms praise Yahweh by recounting his deeds of salvation (e.g. Pss 66:5-7; 71:15-16; 75:1; 77:11-15; 98:1-3; 107:31-32; 145: 4-6). One group of psalms recite Yahweh's mighty deeds in Israel's history to teach us the meaning of our history. They retell the story of God's people to show God's faithfulness, even when his people have erred and strayed from his ways to follow the devices and desires of their own hearts. Psalm 105 presents an historical summary paralleling the Pentateuch from Genesis 12 on. Psalm 106 offers a similar summary recited in a penitential mood. A summary which carries the story up to the selection of David and the choice of Mount Sion (Jerusalem) is found in Psalm 78. Psalm 135 gives an historical summary which includes a reference to Yahweh's power as creator (vss 5-7). Psalm 136 presents an antiphonal summary of Yahweh's great deeds, beginning with creation.

These five psalms recapitulate the unfolding drama of God's dealings with his people from the very beginning of Israel's history to the entrance into the promised land and —in the case of Psalm 78 — as far as the raising up of David as the Anointed One. They recite events fundamental to Israel's self-understanding as a people and central to her knowledge of who God is.

Psalms 135 and 136 associate the story of God's deeds on behalf of Israel with his actions as creator in the beginning. This is true especially of Psalm 136, an historical recitation of God's mighty deeds, in which the congregation makes an antiphonal response to each affirmation: "For his steadfast love endures forever." This is Israel's way of saying that the meaning disclosed in her own historical experience unveils that which underlies the whole of human history right from the start, and indeed of the entire cosmos. The word which God speaks to Israel is the expression of his steadfast love, the same word by which the heavens and the earth were made (Ps 33:6-9).

Israel lives as the manifestation of God's steadfast love. Its life story tells of that love; its worship proclaims it. Israel learned to hear God's word of covenant love in the Exodus events of oppression and deliverance, humiliation and exaltation. Israel lives hearing that word in the concreteness of its life story. Israel's worship summons us to hear that same word in the historical particularities of our story. Its praise is a reflex of the prior action of God which moves his people to "seek his face" (Ps 27:8) within the concrete goodness of their story.

Learning to listen to the word of God within our own life story as a people is at the heart of Israel's spiritual pedagogy. The head of the household in the Jewish Passover liturgy explained the special features of the Passover meal (Ex 12:26) and proclaimed the outline of the story. He recalled the sparing of the houses marked with the blood of the Passover lambs and the redemption out of slavery in Egypt. At the same time he looked forward to redemption in the future, of which the redemption from Egypt was the pattern.

The messiah comes on Passover night when Israel was redeemed and would be redeemed. Memories make the future. Israel looked forward to redemption because it recalled its redemption. The prophetic tradition of Israel had proclaimed that God would send his Messiah to inaugurate a new community "for all peoples," when sorrow and death are things of the past (Is 25:6-8; 65:11-13; Zeph 1:7). The eschatological banquet of universal peace and friendship under God would be achieved by his agent, the messiah. On the basis of the Exodus Israel looked forward to a universal liberation and peace under God. The God that Israel recalled in its present historical experience was the object, embodiment and guarantor of its ultimate hope for salvation. Israel's hope stretches beyond what the present generation experiences; rather, it embraces God's coming in glory, his reign over a new earth, the conversion of Israel and all the nations of the earth, and the new covenant, based on the forgiveness of sins.

Israel trained its people to listen to God in its present experience: "See how God has shown us his glory and his greatness" (Dt 5:24; 11:7). We must pay attention to the wonderful things that God is now doing for us: "The works of God are sublime, deserving the study of those who delight in them" (Ps 111:2). God is actively present in our historical experience, allowing us to celebrate the marvels that he is accomplishing for us (Ps 111:4). If we recognize what God is doing in our life story, we shall be grateful (Ps 111:1) and praise him for his mercy and tenderheartedness (Ps 111:4). We shall proclaim his utter reliability and saving power.

The faithful of Israel feared the condition of death in which there is no knowing God, in the biblical sense. Obliviousness to God's enlivening presence and activity is death in the land of forgetfulness where God no longer works wonders (Ps 88:11). Where all relationships of covenant love with God and neighbor have been forgotten is the condition of death from which the Psalmist seeks deliverance (Ps 88:13). Even now this condition afflicts those who fail to remember God's wonderful works because their relation to the living God has been severed. Having forgotten

God, the dead cannot praise him (Ps 88:11; Is 38:18). They have no life story (of and with God) to share with others. There is no real life where there is no praising of God, and there is no praise where there is no remembering others. Death is the state of absolute aloneness, of oppressive silence apart from God's word and the communication of covenant love (Ps 94:17; 115:17). Those who do not hear God's word are even now experiencing the condition of death. The afflicted Psalmist, expressing a real but partial experience of death (18:5), prays for a life worth living: "Give me life, O Lord, according to your word" (119:107).

Cultic and festive joy characterizes Israel's recognition of God's saving activity in its past and present (e.g. Ps 32:11). Israel's thankful joy before God not only testifies to past experiences of his salvation; it also exults in his faithful dealings which are still future (cf. Hab 3:18) and which believers see ensured by him. Israel's rejoicing embraces the created universe which Israel summons to join in the jubilation (Pss 19:5; 89:12; 96:11). Even God himself rejoices in Israel's jubilation (Is 65:19). Under the prophets both during and after the exile, Israel's rejoicing in its God, even in wretched situations and apparently hopeless moments, broadened out to include anticipatory gratitude for final salvation and messianic joy (Is 61). Israel finds God throughout the entire course of its life story. It responds with exultant rejoicing over God's saving acts in its past, present and eschatological future.

The jubilation that accompanies the dramatic story of Israel finds expression in Mary's Magnificat: "my spirit exults in God my savior" (Lk 1:47). Her exultant rejoicing arises from gratitude and unshakeable trust in the God who has constantly helped and still is helping his people Israel. She has learned from the spiritual pedagogy of her people to recognize and to rejoice in God and what he is doing for his people throughout their entire life story. She rejoices to have been granted a place in his saving purpose for all from Abraham to his descendants for ever (Lk 1:55). She expresses the joy of full participation in the life story of God and his people, a story embracing every generation of humankind that has been blessed by the promise of God to Abraham. Hers is the joy of a people experiencing the fullness of its life story under God with all others; it is not the merely private experience of a solitary visionary or alienated individual. Her life is one with that of all her ancestors and all future generations under God. Therefore, what she receives, they receive; and all generations shall call her is blessed (Lk 1:48). They are blessed through her blessing no less than she is blessed through Abraham's blessing and that of all her ancestors. Mary's listening and telling of what God is speaking and doing for his people within the historical particularities of her life story benefits them just as their listening and telling benefits her; for the same God is blessing his people of every generation.

The Annuniciation is an event within the story of an entire people through and with whom Mary has learned to listen to God and to tell of his saving activity: "Let what you have said be done to me" (Lk 1:38). Mary is the beneficiary of her ancestors' true listening and telling of their story under God. Through their fidelity to the law of listening and telling (*lex narrandi*), she has learned to recognize the same God's saving activity in her experience of the same life story and to put her confidence in him. Her Magnificat celebrates the true goodness of the law of listening and telling for all generations who shall similarly learn through her fidelity to his law to recognize God's saving activity in the past and present and future of their story and, as a consequence, put their confidence in him. The Magnificat expresses the joy of listening and telling that responsible believers know in communicating the goodness of God and his love for all. Rejoicing in listening to God's word and in telling of his saving action that all might put their confidence in him manifests the coming of his kingdom; for his kingdom is coming where his will is being done. Mary finds the joy and meaning of her life in that of a people communicating its faith and hope in God; she shares their responsibility towards God for their past and present and future of authentic listening and truthful telling of his meaning for them. Doing God's will is the joy of his people and the coming of his kingdom.

Israel's listening and telling culminates in that of Jesus. On the mount of transfiguration Jesus' disciples saw his glory and heard the voice saying to them: "Listen to him" (Mt 17:5; Mk 9:7; Lk 9:35). The shepherds' song of praise (*lex orandi*), as well as the confession of the apostles before the Sanhedrin (*lex credendi*), referred to what they had heard and seen (Lk 2:20; Acts 4:20).

Jesus pronounced a blessing on the eyes and ears of those who had become witnesses of the salvation longed for by the faithful of former generations (Mt 13:16; Lk 10:23). To the disciples sent to him by the imprisoned Baptist, Jesus reaffirms Israel's *lex narrandi*: "Go and tell John what you hear and see" (Mt 11:4; Lk 7:22). The disciples, no less than their ancestors, are responsible for remembering to share with others the saving deeds which God is accomplishing in their own day. Recognizing what the God of Israel is doing in the saving words and deeds of Jesus entails their responsibility for proclamation and communication that future generations might continue to believe and hope.

Jesus blesses those who hear and keep his word (Lk 11:28), comparing them to one who builds one's house on rock (Mt 7:24-26). He cites the *Shema* or creed of Israel which declares that the Israelite was to be in daily, constant remembrance of the obligation to love God with one's whole being (Mk 12:29-30): "Listen, O Israel, the Lord our God is one; and you shall love him with all your heart, and with all your soul, and with all your mind, and with all your strength." Jesus hears God as his Father, and as mediator tells what he has heard from him (Jn 8:26; 40; 15:15). He hears his Father in all Israel's life story because it is theirs from start to completion: "I tell you most solemnly, before Abraham ever was, I Am" (Jn 8:58). He affirms: "Your father Abraham rejoiced to think that he would see my Day; he saw it and was glad" (Jn 8:56). What Abraham saw was "from a distance" (cf. Hb 11:13), because he saw it in the birth of the promised Isaac (at which Abraham "laughed", in Gn 17:17), an event prophetic of Jesus, the ultimate meaning of his life story. Jesus claims to be the ultimate meaning and fulfilment of this promise made to Abraham;

he is Isaac according to the spirit. Because Jesus and his Father are the origin, ground, direction, and destiny of Israel's true life story, he accuses those who reject him of having rejected Moses, who had written about him:

> "Do not imagine that I am going to accuse you before the Father: you place your hopes on Moses, and Moses will be your accuser. If you really believed him you would believe me too, since it was I that he was writing about; but if you refuse to believe what he wrote, how can you believe what I say?" (Jn 5:45-47).

Because the love of God is not in them (Jn 3:42), they are simultaneously rejecting Jesus and Moses and God, the life of Israel's true story. Similarly, they are not Abraham's children (Jn 8:39). Israel lives under the sovereignty of God's covenant love; it has no life apart from him. Rejecting that love is rejecting the life that binds Abraham and Moses and Jesus within the one true life story of the people constituted by it. Therefore, Jesus charges his adversaries: "If God were your father, you would love me" (Jn 8:42). They would be bound to Jesus by the same love that bound Abraham and Moses to God. Jesus affirms that his mother and brother and sister — his true "flesh and blood" — are those who hear the word of God and live it; and that they are known as such by their (new) covenant love for one another (Jn 13:35). The true children of Abraham are the brothers and sisters of Jesus and vice versa; they are known as the people living in God's love, which manifests both the accomplishment of his will and the coming of his kingdom. God's word is heard where his love governs the minds and hearts of his people: when the story their life tells is that of his steadfast love for all from Abraham to Moses and Jesus. Such love powerfully summons future generations to hope in God.

Jesus communicates through his listening and telling of the Father's love which is the joy of the people of God. The Father's love for Jesus is the joy of his life and of the people who share it:

> "As the Father has loved me,
> so I have loved you....
> I have told you this so that my own joy may be in you and your joy be complete." (Jn 15:9, 11)

If we accept the gift of the reciprocal love that unites the Father and Jesus and its demand (commandment) for our loving one another as they love one another, we are the friends of Jesus:

> "This is my commandment: love one another, as I have loved you. You are my friends, if you do what I command you." (Jn 15:12, 14)

The joy of the messianic era is known in the friendship of the people whose lives are governed by the same love that united Jesus and his Father. Jesus hears the word of the Father's love for him at the heart of his interpersonal life and communicates what he hears so that an entire people might hear that same word of grace and summons at every level of their life:

> "I call you friends, because I have made known to you everything I have learnt from my Father." (Jn 15:13)

Because the joy which Jesus communicates derives from the gift of his Father's love, it cannot be taken from us (Jn 16:22). The Father loves us for loving his Son (Jn 16:27). Jesus communicates the love that is the joy of his life for the peace of the people who share it: "I have told you all this so that you may find peace in me" (Jn 16:33). Jesus embodies Israel's law of listening and telling for the joy and peace of his people. His fidelity to Israel's *lex narrandi* expresses both God's steadfast love for his people and the perfect response of their love for him. Jesus' life under the sovereignty of his Father's love is shared life with a shared present and past and future. All that he is and does is willingly embraced and undertaken within and for the life of his people, his "flesh and blood." He shares the joy of his covenant love for them to the full (Jn 17:13), so that the love with which the Father loves him may be in them (Jn 17:26). He reveals that that love is available "today."

Luke's Gospel, through its frequent use of the adverb "today" (2:11; 3:22; 4:21; 12:52; 19:5, 9; 23:43), reflects the traditional concern of Israel for recognizing the grace and demand of God's community-creating and sustaining covenant love within the historical particularities of its "today." Israel must hear that word of love "today." The life story of the people for whom Jesus speaks occurs in the "today" of their hearing and communicating his word of the Father's love for all: "And all humankind shall see the salvation of God" (Lk 3:6 = Is 40:5).

The God whose speaking and acting is the life of his people summons all humankind, "today," to assemble with Abraham, Isaac and Jacob in the messianic kingdom, the new Jerusalem (e.g. Is 45:14-17; 49:12; Jer 12:15-16; Mal 1:11; Ps 106). Hearing and communicating the word of his Father's universal love, Jesus affirms that "Men will come from east and west, from north and south, to take their places at the feast in the kingdom of God" (Lk 13:29). The life and story of Israel's God and his people is for all. What makes Israel a people is God's election and grace, and not mere national, natural and historical factors. Jesus affirms that *all* who hear and live the word of God are his mother and brothers and sisters.

At the Last Supper, Jesus affirms that his life is poured out for the life of *all* humankind in the new covenant (Mk 14:24 = Mt 26:28). Through the fulness of his flesh-and-blood relationships with all others, God's saving will is being done and the universal human story is being brought to wholeness and completion (Lk 13:29). The messianic kingdom does not come in a magical, a-personal, a-social, or a-historical way; rather, it comes through the fulness of God's love communicated in the crucified and risen Lord's intra- and interpersonal, social, historical and suprahistorical life for all others.

When Paul writes to churches which consist both of born Jews and born Gentiles, he affirms that all belong to the people of God by faith in Jesus Christ. They are all children of Abraham by virtue of their faith (Rom 4:16-17; cf. Gn 17:5; Gal 3:7; cf. Gn 12:3; Gal 3:13-14, 26-29). The Gentiles who have come to faith in Jesus Christ have been grafted into the rich olive tree of his spiritual and historical heritage, and are supported by it (Rom 11:17). They are no longer outsiders, but part of the family, the "flesh and blood" of Jesus, "where God lives in the Spirit" (Eph 2:19-22). Jesus Christ communicates the fulness of his life to them, making them a part of his own flesh and blood as an individual whose life story is interwoven with that of a family and a people.

Abraham, Isaac, Jacob, Joseph, David, Solomon, Isaiah, Jeremiah, Hosea, Joel, Amos, and Mary, in true covenant love for their own "flesh and blood," have heard the word of God and kept it for Jesus. He does not tell his story of God apart from them; for whatever he hears and communicates from his Father is through his shared present and past and future with his true "flesh and blood." Neither does the Father speak his word nor does the Son enact that word for humankind from outer space; rather, they share their life with their "flesh and blood," where people give themselves in their community-creating and community-sustaining love. Their kingdom is coming where persons dwell in the creative and sustaining love of the Spirit of the Father and Son. Our living in their Spirit is manifested in our loving God and neighbor, in our sharing our life story under the sovereignty of God's love in loving relations with others. Having such life from the author of life is having it more abundantly and sensing the fulness of life in love. This is the joy of the Spirit of the Father and Son sent forth in creation to renew the face of the earth, so that all "flesh and blood" might rejoice in sharing the same life whose story is the good news of Jesus Christ for all.

Our life stories are faithful to the *lex narrandi* when they tell of the God who loves all in the fulness of life that he alone can give. As John said, there is no love of God whom we do not see, if we do not love our neighbor whom we see (1 Jn 1); for in loving God we are to love everyone God loves. Because God loves all, his true "flesh and blood" — all who do his will as the brothers and sisters of Jesus (Mt 12:49-50) — manifest and communicate his love and bear his word of hope for all in the concreteness of their life stories.

When Jesus tells us to take his flesh and blood that we might have eternal life, he is summoning us to participate in the fulness of his interpersonal life with God and all others for the life of the world. He invites us to be sustained by the Father's life in himself as the interpersonal subject communicating that life with all his true "flesh and blood." He pours out his life for all in fulfillment of the promises made to his "flesh and blood" that all humankind may see the salvation of God.

The Lord's Supper is a form of the *lex narrandi* in which Christians remember their obligation of new covenant love to tell of the saving deeds of God on behalf of the "flesh and blood" of his Beloved Son. The Lord's Supper proclaims the Good News that the promise of the new covenant of which both Jeremiah (31:31-33) and Ezechiel (36:26-28) had spoken is now fulfilled for the salvation of all (Zech 2:11-12; 14:16). The Lord's Supper celebrates the fulness of life that God is pouring forth into all his "flesh and blood" in and through Jesus Christ and the gift of their Spirit.

Jesus, the Just One of Israel, assumes responsibility for the past and present and future life of his "flesh and blood." He sends them the Spirit who issues from his Father (Jn 15:25) to teach them everything and remind them of all that he has said to them (Jn 14:26), and to tell them of the things to come (Jn 16:13). Through the gift of his Spirit, Jesus enables his people to grasp the meaning and to cherish the goodness of their past and present and future in the light of his Father's love for them, so that they will forever be able to put their confidence in him. The same Spirit which shaped Jesus' imagination, memory, and anticipation, shapes ours and enables us to tell truthfully his story of God as our own. If we love Jesus we will keep his word (Jn 14:24); if we have his Spirit we are telling his story of his Father's love for all, shaping it within the particularities of our time and place.

When Jesus affirms that we must be nourished by his flesh

and blood to have eternal life (Jn 6:53-58), he is retelling the life story of his people:

> "I tell you most solemnly, it was not Moses who gave you bread from heaven, it was my Father who gives you the bread from heaven, the true bread; for the bread of God is that which comes down from heaven and gives life to the world." (Jn 6:32-33)

The bread of life which the Father gives is the flesh and blood of Jesus "for the life of the world" (Jn 6:51) in an all-inclusive community of new covenant love. The Father is giving his life to all who accept it in the flesh and blood of his Beloved Son. Accepting the flesh and blood of Jesus for eternal life means accepting the promise made to Abraham and its fulfilment in Jesus. It means being forever sustained by the same covenant love of God that is the life which both knew and shared as members of a people. Jesus summons us to make that life ours. Jesus invites all to eat and drink with him, recalling the eschatological banquet for the unity of all humankind under the sovereignty of his Father's sustaining and all-encompassing love. He summons all to accept his heavenly Father, their Holy Spirit, his mother, his Abraham and Isaac and Jacob and Joseph and Moses and David and Isaiah and Jeremiah — all his Jewish flesh and blood with their hope and confidence in God — as our own, for our own sustenance unto eternal life. As the Father nourished and sustained Jesus through his true "flesh and blood" in Israel, he will nourish and sustain us both through them and all others who hear and live according to his word in the community of his covenant love. Jesus sees himself as part of a family and a people that he wills to share with all the families and peoples of the world. The life story of his flesh and blood is for the eternal life of all.

The community of new covenant love gives thanks to the Father for the gift of his eternal life that he is communicating through and in the fulness of his Son's loving interpersonal relation with all others, divine and human, Jew and Gentile, past and present and future. We thank the Father for the love he bears for his Beloved Son in the fulness of his flesh-and-blood relation to all others. We give thanks for our being and our becoming through and in the gift of their Spirit. The Lord's Supper celebrates our belonging to God as his own flesh and blood in his Beloved Son and Spirit. We proclaim the life story of God's own flesh and blood as ours. The interpersonal love of the Triune God — eternal life — is given to us in and through the Jewish flesh and blood of the Beloved Son and his truly human life story with its shared covenant present and past and future. God-made-man is God-made-Jewish in Jesus Christ, the man with a heritage of Jewish hopes for the fulfillment of God's promises to the Jewish people for the salvation of all humankind. God-made-man is God belonging to a people through and in whom we learn that we all belong to one another as his flesh and blood, called to recognize and accept one another as such in the Spirit of his community-creating covenant love for all. The story of God's saving activity of covenant love within the life story of all humankind must be told by his own flesh and blood that all might hope in God: "Do this in memory of me" (Lk 22:19 = 1 Cor 11:24-25).

Any telling of Jesus' story, even though verbally correct, which fails to offer the hearer God's universal covenant love distorts and renders it valueless for that story was created by the gift of God's love to elicit love on all levels of our relations. That story is being truly told where all our relations are being transformed to relations of love rooted and grounded in the life that we receive from our Father in Jesus Christ, which is brought to perfection in the outpouring of their Spirit. Through the gift of the Spirit, we imagine and remember and anticipate with love, the same love that is the life of the Father and Son; we interpret our past and present and future with love; we raise questions with the love that seeks understanding.

The life story of Jesus Christ and his "flesh and blood" in every generation raises questions. Questioning persons are not unwilling learners; rather, as Augustine reminds us, we would not be searching for God had we not already found God. Love *asks* all she meets, as we read in the Song of

Solomon, where she can find her Lover. A loving heart is a questioning heart; an indifferent heart knows no such interest. When Matthew tells the story of Jesus' death he punctuates his narrative with twenty questions. From the anointing of Bethany until the trial before Pilate, Matthew records for us both the questions of Jesus to his enemies and their questioning of him. Even the questions of Jesus' adversaries show that they are not indifferent and are, therefore, at least in touch with the love that could transform them.

Mark's Gospel is called "The beginning of the story of how Jesus Christ, the Son of God, brought the Good News to humankind" (1:1), with the implication that the story is still in the process of being told by his true "flesh and blood," who live in his Spirit, and has not yet reached its culmination in the resurrection of the just and the fulness of the kingdom of God. The memory and aspirations of Jesus are being kept alive by the community that lives in his Spirit.

The four Gospel writers keep the memory and anticipations of Jesus alive by telling his story. Their stories reflect their experience of what it means to be the friends of God living in the Spirit of his Beloved Son. The writers creatively use their imaginations in remembering to share their story of God with others. Motivated by their kerygmatic concern to persuade their hearers to accept and live in the Spirit of Jesus Christ and his Father, the evangelists enriched and reshaped their memories of Jesus' words and deeds by drawing upon the images available to them. They constructed dramatic narratives in which the images of the Hellenistic world and especially the images of the Old Testament served to articulate their call to conversion, to "remember God" in the crucified and risen Christ and his Spirit. The Messiah, the Lord, the Son of Man, the Good Shepherd — each image placed at the service of Christian faith a wealth of symbolic power evoking the meaning incarnate in Jesus and eliciting the affections of their hearers. Through their dramatic narratives and images the evangelists give rise to insights into the identity of the ultimate source and term of their love with the Father of Jesus, the God of Israel who has sent his Beloved Son. Jesus, the revelation and image (icon) of the Father, completes his mission by sending the Spirit. Thus the four evangelists symbolize the realm of the transcendent in Trinitarian imagery, intrepreting the God who is transforming their lives in terms of interpersonal love. The four narratives communicate four distinctive and complementary aspects of the Christian community's experience and understanding of that love. They are four icons of the God who is Love. They are a fourfold norm for discerning whether or not we are even beginning to live in the Spirit of Jesus Christ.

In remembering to share their story of God, the four Evangelists have communicated their experience of his steadfast (new) covenant love and trust-worthiness that all might put their confidence in him. They respond to the word that God speaks within their life story by becoming the communicators of faith and hope for others. They communicate complementary aspects of the grace and demand of that word for authentic human development and fulfillment under the sovereignty of God's love. The costly commitment of Christians to God in the service of others both within the realm of family responsibilities and the world beyond is rooted and grounded in the mutual indwelling and self-transcending love of the Father and Son that constitutes the community of Christian faith. The outgoing compassion of Christians for others without limits or conditions bears witness to the indwelling Trinitarian love that is the ultimate source and term of the Christian community's life and that of the world it is called to serve.

Although all Christians are called by the gift of the Spirit to share their story of God for building up the faith and hope of others (*lex narrandi*), the Christian community of faith has made the four gospel stories normative for ascertaining the authenticity of our stories of God and of our claims to be the friends of God in Jesus Christ and his Spirit. The story of true friends of God will always be one of self-transcendence in a costly commitment to the service of others both within and outside the Christian community. If we have never willingly undergone inconvenience or suffering in our commitment to God and neighbor, we probably have never taken either seriously. The love that has its origin and term in God takes others seriously. There is no authentically Christian story without the lived knowledge of the paschal mystery of dying to ourselves to rise to new life with others under the sovereignty of God's love for all in Christ and his Spirit. There is no such story without the costly commitment of new covenant love to the "flesh and blood," the brothers and sisters, of Jesus Christ. The disciple shares the master's commitment of covenant fidelity to his people. Just as the Father nourished and sustained his Beloved Son through and in his true "flesh and blood" in Israel, he nourishes and sustains us through and in the brothers and sisters of Jesus Christ. We cannot know Jesus, in the biblical sense of knowing, apart from his brothers and sisters. Sharing Jesus' loving relations with them is sharing his life of family responsibility before the Father. Such life does not exclude those outside the family; for all human persons are called to become the brothers and sisters of Jesus Christ. His life is in the service of all, so that "all humankind shall see the salvation of God" (Lk 3:6 = Is 40:5). *All* who hear and keep the word of God are his brothers and sisters. His outgoing love of compassion for all tells the story of his Father's universal love and saving will for all. There is no truly Christian story of God that does not entail the costly commitment of compassionate love for the world, for all, for enemies, for strangers, for all "the others." No true friend of God is indifferent to them.

There is no authentic telling of the story of Jesus apart from his own mystical experience of his Father and their Spirit given to us. The Father and the Spirit are at the heart of his intrapersonal life. The unity of Christians is rooted in this mutual indwelling love; for theirs is the love that we have for one another. In our mutual indwelling love for one another we share the mystical experience that Jesus has of his Father and their Spirit given to us. We share the vocation of Jesus to manifest and communicate that love in the service of all. We share his prayer for all (*lex orandi*) "that the love with which you (Father) have loved me may be in them, and I in them" (Jn 17:26); that is, that the Spirit of love who is in Jesus be in all others.

APPENDIX[1]

Theses for a Theology of Story

A. A Phenomenology of Storytelling

1   Human beings as the subjects of their stories.

1.1 People are storytelling animals.

1.2 People are storymaking animals.

1.3 The self is conscious as the subject of a verb.

    1.31   The self is a particular agent that is known and revealed in its life story.

    1.311 Every human life story shares the three temporal dimensions of past, present, and future, which are respectively called to mind by memory, awareness, and anticipation.

    1.312 The meaning of (life) stories is seen from the end.

    1.3121 Human stories involve both a process (promise) and a term (fulfillment).

    1.3122 The beginning of a human story is the promise of its ending or fulfillment.

---

[1]The following theses appear in my book, coauthored with Thomas Cooper: *Tellers of the Word* (Le Jacq Inc., 53 Park Place, New York, N.Y. 10007).

1.3123 We organize our storymaking around the conclusion that we have chosen for our stories, or around what we believe must be their conclusion.

1.4 The art of storytelling expresses the art of living.
    1.41 A condition for sanity is the ability to tell our stories

1.5 What human life stories mean to us depends on what kind of person we are.
    1.51 Human life stories are their own interpretation inasmuch as they are the product of the understanding that people have of themselves, their situation, their role, the human condition. The interpretation interprets the interpreter.
    1.52 Of the symbols with which we spontaneously but uncritically express our life story, a privileged place is occupied by parental imagery.
    1.521 These spontaneous symbols, because they are spontaneous, are in need of critical reflection.

1.6 Our storylistening prepares us for our storymaking: we are storylisteners before we become storytellers.

1.7 There are two poles to the horizon of every story.

1.8 Human security is grounded in the stories we hear and tell.
    1.81 The movement from one stage of storytelling to another stage, accompanied by the threat to the subject's sense of security, is confirmed as a law of human development by the developmental psychologies of Erikson and Kohlberg.
    1.82 The story told by a human life is not exclusively a story of peak experiences.
    1.821 Patience is a precondition for all divine and human storymaking.

2   The craft of telling stories.

2.1 Like a teacher, a craftsperson, or an artist, the storyteller must use techniques and skills adapted for his or her purpose.
- 2.11 We cannot do what we cannot, at least in some way, imagine or envision.
- 2.111 Authentic lives evidence authentic vision.
- 2.12 The art of the storyteller is measured by his or her ability to master complexity: the more that he or she is able to unify within his or her story, the greater his or her art as a storyteller.
- 2.121 The excellence of human stories is measured by the demands they make of their authors.

2.2 The storyteller is implicitly a teacher inasmuch as she or he creates a story that moves the listener to decision.
- 2.21 Stories are a mutual creation of the teller and the listeners.

2.3 The author of a story has an attitude toward the subject of the story.
- 2.31 The author of a story has an attitude toward his or her audience.

2.4 The true meaning and value of human stories are determined by their context.

2.5 There is no human story without limits.

2.6 The human action that defines a story is a declaration of a basic faith.
- 2.61 We seek to live by the stories that embody our basic faith.
- 2.611 Since the communication and expression of faith transcends all conceptual knowledge, both its expression and communication lie in the symbolic mode of consciousness, symbol being defined as the best possible expression of an unknown content.
- 2.6111 Because the symbolic is rooted in the psychic depths of the personality there is need of a

critical mediation of symbols. Because the critical intellect can never comprehend the mystery of God, there is a need for a return to the symbolic.

2.62 Images, and the stories that contain them, provide models and motives for the decisions and actions that shape our lives.

2.621 Human conduct is more story or model abiding than it is principle or law abiding.

2.6211 Law-abiding behavior can itself be a mode of storytelling.

2.63 A human life story is not exclusively a matter of self-determination.

3 The meaning of human stories.

3.1 That every person who has ever lived out a story of storytelling and storylistening posits a comprehensible universe with a permanent meaning at the heart of things.

    3.11 Stories express the horizon of their author's vision.

    3.12 Human stories are implicit answers to the fundamental questions that arise concerning life and death.

    3.13 Human stories raise questions about the answers that they imply with regard to the basic questions about life and death.

3.2 God is ultimately intended by every human life story.

B. The Universal Story of God Told in the Life Story of Jesus

4 God is revealed through human stories.

4.1 God is a particular agent that is known and revealed in his story.

4.11 The transcendent Spirit of God is, and is known, where it acts in the self-transcending faith and hope and love through which it transforms our lives.
4.12 Inasmuch as God is the giver of all human life stories, they are manifestations of his grace and are measured by the demands of his intention.
4.13 Human stories are implicitly coauthored with God and neighbor.

4.2 The story in which God is known and revealed is the Word of God.
4.21 The universal story, together with every human life story, is God's primary word.
4.22 The stories of God told by prophets, priests, apostles, evangelists, and others are secondary word.

4.3 Jesus the Storyteller redeems all human storytelling.
4.31 Every human life story will reflect the presence of evil in the world and in men's lives.
4.311 The guilt that attends every life story must not only be experienced but also understood and judged.
4.312 Guilt is not absolved by observing that the person "meant well."
4.32 As storymaking animals we are responsible for our failure to tell our story authentically.
4.33 The true meaning and value of a human story are precarious; they can be lost through a misinterpretation of the meaning and a noncommitment to its value.
4.331 Sin consists in the deliberate distortion of our life stories in order to take them out of their proper context in the universal story.
4.34 Jesus Christ's making and telling of stories summon all humankind to share his filial responsibility for the making of their stories.
4.341 The divine Storymaker unifies all creation within his universal story.

4.4 The way in which we envision God is always determined from the start by the way we love and treasure the things presented to us within the context of our life's story.

    4.41 The way that Jesus Christ loved and treasured the things presented to him within the context of his life story reveals to Christian faith the meaning of authentic love and the true vision of God.

4.5 The meaning of Jesus Christ is seen as the outcome of his life story.

    4.51 The vision of the Beloved Sonship symbolized in the baptism of Jesus is further revealed as the foundation of the Christian story by Jesus' Way of the Cross.

    4.52 The story of Christ's life reveals the necessity of suffering in every human life story.

    4.521 The Way of the Cross as disclosed in the story of Jesus reveals the nature of authentic suffering.

    4.522 The cross reveals to Christian faith the extent to which the divine Storymaker is committed to the excellence of his universal story.

4.6 Because our faith is preconceptual our telling and listening to God's story will be a communion of the incommunicable and an expression of the inexpressible.

    4.61 The symbols with which we spontaneously express the life story of God are taken from our own unthematized expression of our life story.

5 The gift of God's love through the Holy Spirit of Jesus Christ grounds the story of Christian conversion.

5.1 The telling and the hearing of the Gospel story are the work of the same Spirit working in both the teller and the hearer.

    5.11 Christian conversion is a gift of God that enables us to hear the story of Jesus and his Church.

Appendix 149

    5.12   Christian conversion is a gift of God that enables us to tell the story of Jesus and his Church.

5.2 The materials of the Gospel story point to distinctive understanding of God's gift of his love manifested in Jesus and to the dimensions of discipleship associated with them.
    5.21   In appropriating the story told by the four Gospels we appropriate our own life story.
    5.22   The Gospel story calls its hearers to return (be converted) to themselves in the process of being converted to God.

5.3 Four versions of the Gospel story serve the Church as four manuals for the attainment of Christian maturity.
    5.31   The story as told by Mark prepares the catechumen for the sacramental celebration of the first moment of conversion.
    5.32   The story as told by Matthew illuminates the way for the newly baptized to enter into fellowship.
    5.33   The story as told by Luke, both in his Gospel and in Acts, aids the newly converted and mutually strengthened Christian to enter into a life of missionary commitment.
    5.34   The story as told by John serves the mature and contemplative Christian as a manual for ascertaining and attaining the full development of the Christian life.
    5.35   Bernard Lonergan's theology of conversion allows us to understand the progressive unfolding of the Chrisian story from Mark through John.

5.4 The death of Jesus outside the "camp" or "city" symbolizes Christian conversion as a breakout from our self-imposed imprisonment.
    5.41   The Church employs the four stories of Mark, Matthew, Luke and John as a means for communicating and cultivating its foundational

experience of the love of God in Christ Jesus and in his Spirit that has been given us.

5.42 Basic to our experience of conversion is the felt judgment that we are loved.

5.421 The world disclosed by Jesus in his Sonship of God defines each Christian storyteller as one who has been trusted.

5.43 The different ways of telling the story of Jesus correspond to the diverse ways in which God can tell us that we are loved.

5.431 The names of Jesus connote the ways that God's gift of his love transforms our lives and constitutes the life story of the church.

5.5 Christian conversion is worked out in a process of self-transcendence, in a lifetime's death in love and self-surrender.

    5.51 The truths of the Gospel story evoke Christian conversion both as event and as process.

    5.52 The division of the Scriptures into Old and New Testaments and the story of Jesus as told by Luke-Acts symbolize the presence of continuity and discontinuity in stories of Christian conversion.

    5.53 The story of Jesus being in agony in the garden discloses the inescapable presence of tension in the life of Christian conversion.

5.6 Christian conversion is sacramentally signified by the grace of matrimony.

    5.61 The charism of celibacy for the Kingdom reflects the narrative quality of our life in Christ.

5.7 The story of Judas as portrayed by the Gospel writers discloses ultimate human failure as the betrayal of the divine offer of friendship.

6   Jesus Christ is the Sacrament who transforms human life stories.

6.1 The categories appropriate to a critical understanding of the Gospel story are aesthetic rather than classically scientific.
- 6.11 The claim to universal validity of the judgment of taste provides a fruitful analogy for understanding the claim to universal validity made by the Gospel story.
- 6.12 The claim to universal validity implicit in the judgment of taste provides a fruitful if imperfect analogy for understanding how, through the Incarnation, we love the God whom no human eye has seen.

6.2 Human life stories function as icons of the divine life story.
- 6.21 The life story of every human storyteller functions as an icon of that storyteller's faith.
- 6.22 The life story of the crucified-risen Jesus is the primordial sacrament of God's gift of his love, experienced by the Christian as underlying and informing all human life stories.
- 6.23 The Gospel stories function as sacramental symbols evoked by the feeling for Christ of their writers and evoking the feeling for Christ of their readers or listeners.
- 6.24 The Resurrection is the key to the Christian interpretation of the divine and human coauthoring of the Jesus story, the story of the Church and the universal story of the world.

7 The Jesus story as foundation for the story of his community, the Church

7.1 Persons communicate and relate to one another by the stories they tell.
- 7.11 There can be no community life, no consensus, and thus no common action without participation in a common understanding of the meaning of a common story and without common

commitment to that story's value.
- 7.12 The life story of a community is the common good of those who call to mind its meaning and value by memory, awareness, and anticipation.
- 7.13 The tradition of a community or society is the story of its life.
- 7.14 Authentic storytelling is the creation of a community of love.

7.2 The members of a society benefit from its common story only to the extent that they allow themselves to be governed by it.
- 7.21 Every society has limits to its tolerance for the diversity of its members' interpretations of its common (foundational) story.

7.3 Preparation is required for grasping the meaning of human stories.
- 7.31 Our experience of the Jesus story is conditioned by our experience of the world.
- 7.32 Our understanding of the Jesus story, the Good News, is conditioned by our participation in the living communities of Christian faith that tell the story.
- 7.33 The tradition of the Church is the life story of Christians.

8 The Jesus story reveals that human beings are ever to be "surprised by joy."

8.1 The Gospel stories witness the amazing quality of God's grace.

8.2 Christ's story of the Good Samaritan challenges our a priori assumptions about the mode in which God will reveal himself to us.

9 The Blessed Trinity and Undivided Unity of God is the beginning, the middle, and the end of all our storytelling.

Appendix 153

9.1 The mystery of the Blessed Trinity and Undivided Unity symbolically present in human consciousness, points to God as the deepest fulfillment of the human Spirit.

9.2 The human experience of telling and listening to stories provides a fruitful if imperfect analogy for the Blessed and Undivided Trinity.

9.3 The interpersonal dynamics of the life story of Jesus Christ as disclosed in his life of universal friendship function as a fruitful model for understanding the interpersonal dynamics of our life in Christ.

9.4 The interpersonal life of Jesus Christ — his relationships to God and to his fellow humans, to divine and human persons — is the prime analogate for the Christian community's experience and understanding and judgment of its own interpersonal relationships with divine and human persons, and to the relationship between the universal story and the Blessed Trinity.

OLD TESTAMENT INDEX

Genesis
12:3   136
17:5   136
17:17   132
37:3   95

Exodus
1:16   55, 56
3:6   61
4:22-23   73
6:6   56
7:4   56
10:2   56
10:21-23   55
10:23   79
11:5   55
12:13   53
12:26   128
17:7   77, 86
33:11   58
33:14   58

Leviticus
17:10-16   49
21:10   95
23:42-44   76

Deuteronomy
5:4   125
5:24   129
6—8   85
6:4   52
6:10-13   123
8:2   123
8:5   123
8:17-19   86
8:18   123
8:19   123

11:7   129
12:23   49

1 Kings
8:6   61
8:10   61

2 Chronicles
36:18   61

Ezra
13:4   62

Job
18:21   29

Psalms
2:7   63
18:5   130
19:5   130
21[22]   57, 58, 65, 94, 95, 97, 98
21[22]:1   54, 56
21[22]:24   98
27:8   128
31[30]:5   83, 85
31:24   125
32:11   130
33:6-9   128
41[42]:2   96
62[63]:3   96
66:5-7   127
68[69]   57
71:15-16   127
75:1   127
78   127, 128
78:70   125
78:72   125

78:177   124
88:11   129, 130
88:13   129
89:12   13
94:17   130
95:6   126
96:11   130
97:10   125
98:1-3   127
105   127
106   127, 135
107:31-32   127
111:1   129
111:2   129
111:4   129
115:17   130
119:107   130
130:7   126
135   125, 127
136   127, 128
145:4-6   127

Song of Solomon
2:16   125

Isaiah
11:4   62
25:6-8   129
38:18   130
40:5   122, 135
42:1   64
42:6   69
45:14-17   135
49:12   135
52   57
53   57
53:7   79
53:9   79

53:12	106	**Daniel**		**Amos**	
61	130	12:2	69	8:9	54, 67
65:11-13	129				
65:19	130	**Hosea**		**Habakkuk**	
		11:9	126	3:18	130
Jeremiah					
2:5	29	**Joel**			
12:15-16	135	3:1-2	66	**Zephaniah**	
15:9	54	3:3-5	66	1:7	129
22:15-16	29	4:1-8	66		
31:2	125	4:9-14	66		
31:31-33	137	4:10-21	66	**Zechariah**	
		4:14-17	69	2:11-12	137
Ezekiel		4:15-16	67		
16:1-9	89	4:16	67	**Malachi**	
16:8-9	89	4:17	69	1:2	125
36:26-28	137	27:45	67	1:11	135
37:12-14	67	27:51-53	67		

NEW TESTAMENT INDEX

Matthew		5:34	104	12:24-29	74
1:20	73	5:39	104	12:24	74
1:21	44, 66, 73	5:43-44	41	12:26	74
1:22-23	32	5:44	104	12:27	74
1:23	31, 32, 74	5:45	31	12:34	36, 37
2:1-12	68	5:48	39	12:49-50	137
2:6	73	6:1	75	12:49	31
2:15	32, 73	6:10	73, 74	12:50	31, 73, 95
3:1—4:11	106	6:13	74	13:9	74
3:16-17	32, 73	7:21-23	104	13:16	132
3:17	32, 73	7:21	73	13:17	68
4:1-11	73, 74, 85	7:23	37, 74	13:19	74
4:3-4	73	7:24-26	132	13:38	31
4:3	74	8:17	38	13:39	74
4:5-7	73	9:36	39	13:41	74
4:5	69	10:24-25	32, 106	13:43	74
4:8-10	73	10:34-35	74	14:14	39
4:12—18:35	106	11:3-6	74	14:33	32, 70
4:17	74	11:4	132	15:7	37
5:7	40	11:14-15	74	15:22	40
5:9	31	11:18-19	40	15:32	39
5:16	35	11:20-21	37	16:16	32, 70
5:17	69	11:20	74	16:21	106
5:22	104	11:25-27	31	16:23	74
5:28	104	11:27	32	17:5	32, 132
5:32	104	11:29	32	17:12	106

17:15	40	28:10	31	10:21	41
17:21-23	106	28:18	104	10:27	19, 112
18:1-7	35	28:19-20	31	10:32-34	59, 106
18:3	32	28:19	32	10:43-45	31
18:4	75	28:20	32	10:45	38, 44, 49
18:6	32			11—16	106
18:10	32, 35			11—12	111
18:14	73	**Mark**		11:15-19	59
18:20	31, 32	1:1-13	106	11:15-17	37
18:21	31	1:1	64, 140	11:17	62
18:27	39	1:4	66	11:21	37
18:32-33	40	1:10	62	11:27	111
18:33	39	1:11	61, 62, 64	11:36	19
18:35	31	1:12-13	85	12:1-11	55
19:1—20:34	106	1:14—9:50	106	12:12-27	59
19:26	19, 112	1:14—3:6	111	12:13-17	111
20:17-19	106	1:15	31, 112	12:18-27	111
20:25-28	32	1:17	107	12:28-34	111
20:28	38, 49, 50	1:22	104	12:29-30	132
20:30-31	40	1:41	38	12:38-40	59
21—28	106	1:43	37	13:1-2	59
21:12-13	37	2:1—3:5	111	13:1	107
21:31-32	74	2:7	64	13:5-6	61
21:43	35	3:5	36, 37, 38	13:33-37	52
23:8	31	3:6	111	13:35	51
23:12	75	3:7—6:6	111	14—15	104
23:13-36	37	3:21	111	14:21	80
23:28	74	3:35	95	14:23ff	49
23:33	36	4:40	37	14:24	17, 31, 44, 49, 62, 66, 135
24:12	74	6:4	111		
24:51	37	6:6—8:33	111	14:33	38
25:31-46	40, 109	6:6	111	14:34	38
25:37	109	6:34	39	14:35-36	57
25:46	109	6:50	61	14:36	65, 112
26—27	104	8:2	39, 107	14:37	30, 51
26:24	80	8:17	111	14:58	59, 60
26:27-29	49	8:22-26	107	14:61	59
26:28	17, 44, 50, 66, 70, 135	8:31-32	106	14:62	61
		8:31	65, 107, 111	15:5	78
26:37-38	38	8:33	37, 111	15:16-20	18
26:37	38	8:34-35	30, 106	15:23	53
26:39	75	8:35	107	15:25	50
26:63	70	9:2-7	65	15:29	59
26:63-64	32	9:7	61, 64, 112, 132	15:32	59
27:40	70, 74			15:33	50, 54
27:43	70	9:12	106	15:34	30, 54, 56, 67
27:46	38	9:23	39	15:36	34
27:50	67	9:31-32	106	15:37-39	62
27:52-53	67	9:42	37	15:37	58, 59
27:52	68	10:1-52	106	15:38	58, 59
27:53	69	10:14	37	15:39	45, 58, 59, 63, 81
27:54	32, 70	10:16	37		

Luke

1:19	60
1:38	131
1:47	130
1:48	131
1:54	39
1:55	130
1:58	39
1:71	39
1:72	39
1:78	39
2:11	135
2:20	132
2:49	77
3:1—4:13	
3:3	66
3:6	40, 122, 135, 142
3:22	135
4:1-13	73, 85
4:3	86
4:5-7	77
4:13	78
4:14—9:50	106
4:18	108
4:21	135
4:43	77
5:1-11	33
5:29-32	33, 40
5:29-30	40
5:32	40
5:48	32
6:22	106
6:27	81
6:32-34	33
6:35	32, 33
6:36	32, 39, 81
7:13	39
7:22	132
7:33	40
7:36-50	40
7:36-38	33
7:36	41
8:1-3	41
8:21	95
9	135
9:10-17	39
9:22	106
9:31	44, 76
9:35	132
9:41	37
9:43-45	106
9:51—19:57	77
9:51—18:43	106
9:51-55	33
9:51	76
10:13	37
10:23	132
10:25	33
10:29-37	33
10:30-37	33
10:33	39
10:37	39
10:38-42	41
11:5-8	41
11:28	132
11:37	41
12:4	40
12:46	37
12:52	135
13:23	33
13:27	37
13:29	33, 135
13:30	33
13:33	77
14:1	41
14:26-27	106
15	37
15:1-2	33, 39, 40
15:20	39
17:11-19	33
17:25	77, 106
18:9-14	33, 40
18:27	19, 112
18:31-34	106
19—24	106
19:1-10	33, 40
19:5-7	33
19:5	135
19:30	84
19:41	38
19:45-46	37
21:13-14	78
22—23	104
22:3	78
22:19	139
22:20	17, 49
22:28-29	41, 115
22:28	78
22:31	78
22:32	78
22:37	38, 77
22:42	75
22:44	38
22:52	79, 85
22:53	44, 79
22:61-62	40
23:4	78
23:9	79
23:11	78
23:14-15	78
23:14	78
23:15	78
23:22	78
23:34	81
23:39-43	33
23:41	78
23:42	81
23:43	81, 135
23:44	83
23:45	80
23:46	38, 83
23:47	78, 80, 82, 83
23:48	82
24:1-6	84
24:26	84
24:25-26	37
24:51	76

John

1:1-18	46
1:12	48, 105
1:19—12:50	46
2:4	95
2:11	46
2:13-17	37
2:25	108
3:5	93
3:13	75
3:14-15	87
3:14	44, 87, 92
3:16-17	46, 92, 116
3:16	93
3:17	46
3:35	43
3:42	133
4:34	88, 89
4:42	46
5:19-20	43
5:45-47	133
6:32-33	138
6:51	87, 93, 138
6:53-58	138
6:53-55	49
7:39	91, 92
7:40	47

7:43	95	14:15-16	34	18:1—20:31	87
8:26	132	14:16	91	18:4	87
8:28	44, 87, 92	14:21	92	18:6	87
8:39	133	14:23	43	18:8-9	87
8:42	133	14:24	92	18:11	87
8:55	111-112	14:24	137	18:20-24	87
8:56	132	14:25	47	18:38	87
8:58	132	14:26	86, 91, 92, 137	19:2-3	86
9:16	95			19:9	87
10:1-18	87	14:31	89	19:10-11	87
10:10	48	15:5	34	19:23	95
10:11	89	15:9	34, 134	19:24	94
10:14-15	43	15:9-10	92	19:25	95
10:15	42	15:9-13	116	19:26-27	95
10:19	95	15:10	92	19:26	42
10:25-30	94	15:10-11	114	19:28-30	90
11	93	15:11	113, 134	19:28	96
11:1-44	90	15:12-16	42	19:30	90, 92, 94
11:3	41, 93	15:12	18, 28, 34, 134	19:31-37	96
11:5	41, 93			20:2	42
11:11	42	15:13	18, 34, 35, 42, 88, 89, 92, 108, 134	20:17	92
11:14-15	93			20:21-23	92
11:24	93			20:22	91
11:26	93	15:13-15	93	20:29	47
11:34	42	15:14	42	20:30	46
11:35	38	15:14	134	20:31	33, 44
11:36	42	15:15	34, 89, 115, 132	21:7	42
11:50	94			21:20	42, 47
11:51-52	94	15:18-26	87	40	132
12:16	92	15:20	111-112		
12:23-26	106	15:25	137		
12:24	87	15:26	91, 92	**Acts**	
12:32	44, 75, 87, 92, 96	16:6-11	91	1:1-9	84
		16:13	86, 91, 137	2	82
13:1—20:31	46	16:13-14	93	4:20	132
13:1	42, 46, 87, 88, 92	16:22	114, 134	7:9-11	95
		16:26-27	93	7:59-60	81
13:7	28	16:27	134	7:59	84
13:10	88	16:28	46, 87	10:45	17
13:14-15	109	16:33	134		
13:15	88	17:1	86		
13:17	109	17:2	104	**Romans**	
13:27	42	17:3	33, 87, 89, 90	1:18	37
13:33-36	42	17:4	88, 89	4:16-17	136
13:34-35	116	17:5	92	5:5	17
13:34	28, 42	17:12	87	5:11	115
13:35	34, 133	17:13	114, 135	6:1-14	27
14—17	86	17:20	43	8:12-13	27
14:6	46	17:21	34, 92	8:32	57
14:8-9	46	17:23	92	11:7	136
14:9	47	17:26	92, 135, 142	12:19-21	27
14:10	34	18—19	104	14:1—15:7	27

1 Corinthians		Ephesians		10:19-20	58
1:21	23	1:7	66	11:13	132
2:2	110	2:19-22	136		
3:18-19a	103	5:2	57		
5:7-8	27	5:25	57	**1 Peter**	
6:9-12	27			3:18	57
6:15-20	17	**Philippians**			
7	27	1:9ff	28		
11:24-25	139				
11:25-27	49	**Colossians**		**1 John**	
13:7	110	1:14	66	1	136
13:12	110	1:24	113	1:1-4	43
15:3	66	2:24	79	1:1-3	41
15:20	68			1:1	43
		1 Timothy		1:4	43
Galatians		2:6	50	2:3-5	29
1:4	79			2:3	29
3:7	136	**Titus**		3:18	103, 121
3:13-14	136	3:4	41, 115	4:8	28, 43, 105
3:26-29	136			4:11	28
4:9	110	**Hebrews**		4:16	43, 105
5:13-14	27	2:4	79	4:21	28
6:4-5	103	9:22	66	5:6-7	96

AUTHOR INDEX

Anderson, B., 20

Bradshaw, P. F., 20
Brown, R. E., 21

Cooper, Thomas, 20, 143
Crowe, Frederick E., 105

Dych, William V., 107

Erikson, 144

Fitzmyer, J. A., 21

George, Augustin, 110
Grelot, Pierre, 110
Groomer, T. H., 20

Hefling, Charles, 105

Kelber, W. H., 20
Kiely, Bartholomew, 116
Kingsbury, J. D., 20
Kohlberg, 144

Léon-Dufour, Xavier, 20, 110

Liverani, B., 110
Lonergan, Bernard, 12, 105, 149

Martinez, Ernest, 19, 20
Mastrandrea, A., 110
Murphy, R. E., 21

Navore, J., 20

Rahner, Karl, 12-13, 14
Reumann, John, 111

Segal, J. B., 20
Selby, Donald, 20, 71

Trocmé, E., 20

Vanhoye, Albert, 19-20

Weber, J. C., Jr., 111
Wilder, Amos, 22
Winter, Paul, 111
Wittgenstein, 15

Zedda, S., 21

DATE DUE			
NOV 28 '85			
FEB 12 '86			
DEC 18 '87			
JY 15 '91			
DE 26 '91			
NO 2 '98			
AP 28 '99			
MY 08 '99			
MAY 21 1999			

```
BT                    104146
78
.N3       Navone, John J.
1984         Gospel love :
```

HIEBERT LIBRARY
Fresno Pacific College - M. B. Seminary
Fresno, Calif. 93702